PANAMA
Made in the USA

John Weeks and Phil Gunson

Latin America
Bureau

ii

First published in 1991 in Great Britain by the Latin America Bureau
(Research and Action) Ltd, 1 Amwell Street, London EC1R 1UL

British Library Cataloguing in Publication Data

Weeks, John
    Panama : made in the USA.
    1. Panama. Foreign relations with United States 2. United States. Foreign relations with
    Panama
    I. Title II. Gunson, Phil
    327.7287073

ISBN 0 906156 55 6 pbk
ISBN 0 906156 56 4 hbk

Written by John Weeks and Phil Gunson
Additional research by Bob Carty, Charlotte Elton and
Edward Orlebar
Edited by Duncan Green

Cover photo by Bill Robinson/*The Observer*
Cover design by Andy Dark

Typeset, printed and bound by Russell Press, Nottingham NG7 4ET
Trade distribution in UK by Central Books, 99 Wallis Road, London E9 5LN
Distribution in North America by Monthly Review Press, 122 West 27th Street, New
York, NY 10001

Printed on recycled, straw-based paper.

Contents

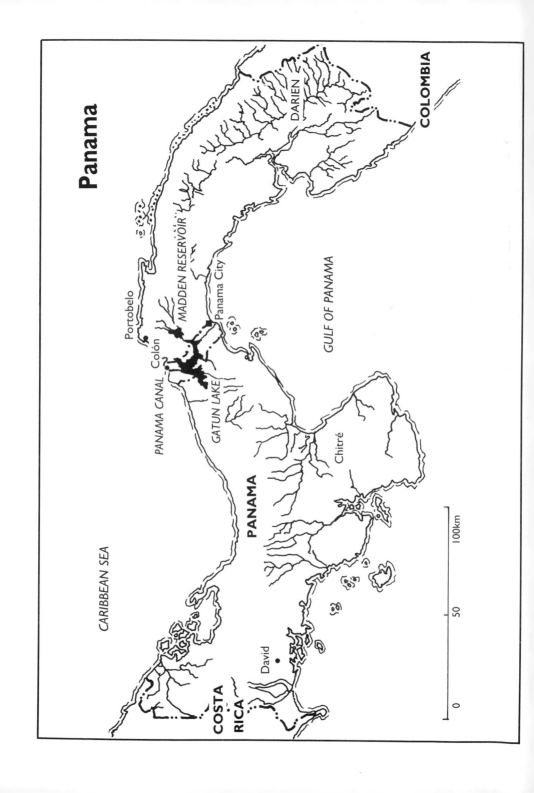

Panama

COLOMBIA

DARIEN

CARIBBEAN SEA

Portobelo

Colón

PANAMA CANAL

MADDEN RESERVOIR

Panama City

GATUN LAKE

PANAMA

GULF OF PANAMA

Chitré

David

COSTA
RICA

0   50   100km

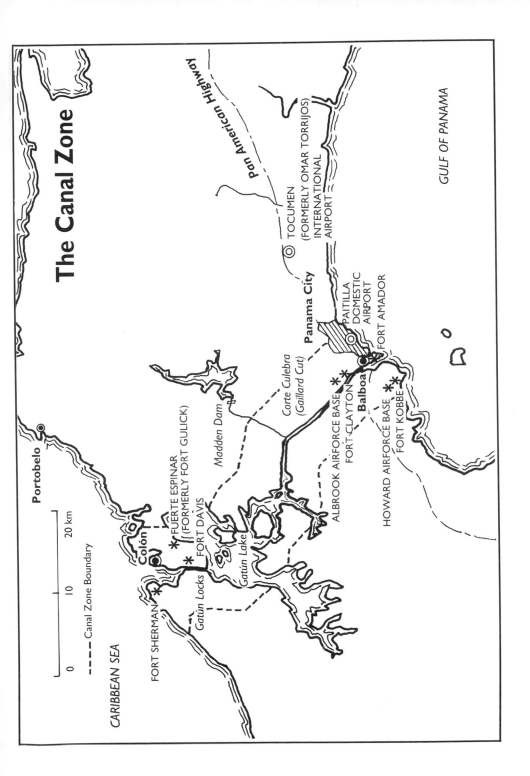

The Canal Zone

CARIBBEAN SEA

Portobelo

Colón

FORT SHERMAN

Gatún Locks

FUERTE ESPINAR
(FORMERLY FORT GULICK)
FORT DAVIS

Gatún Lake

Madden Dam

Corte Culebra
(Gaillard Cut)

ALBROOK AIRFORCE BASE
FORT CLAYTON

Balboa

FORT AMADOR

HOWARD AIRFORCE BASE
FORT KOBBE

Panama City

PAITILLA
DOMESTIC
AIRPORT

TOCUMEN
(FORMERLY OMAR TORRIJOS)
INTERNATIONAL
AIRPORT

Pan American Highway

GULF OF PANAMA

0   10   20 km

— — — Canal Zone Boundary

Panama in Brief

Country and People

Area	77,000 sq km
Population (1989)	2.37 million
Urban	54%
Rural	46%
Ethnic Composition	
Mestizo	70%
Afro-Caribbean	14%
White	9%
Indian	7%
Religion	
Catholic	86%
Protestant	12%
Unemployment (1988)	21%
Health	
Life Expectancy (1987)	
Female	74
Male	70
Infant Mortality (1987)	
p/1000 live births	23
Maternal Mortality (1980)	
p/100,000 live births	90
Literacy (1986)	85.8%

Economy

Gross Domestic Product (GDP, 1988)	$4,518 million
GDP per capita	$1,964

Date	% growth/decline in GDP
1985	4.7
1986	3.4

1987	2.3
1988	-17.8
1989 (est)	-1.2

Distribution of GDP
Agriculture	9%
Industry	18%
Services	73%

| Total External Debt (1989) | $6,800 million |

Trade (1989, including imports and re-exports to Colón Free Zone)
| Imports | $3,185 million |
| Exports | $2,723 million |

Principal Exports (1988, excluding Colón Free Zone re-exports)
Bananas	$76.5 million
Shrimp	$51.8 million
Sugar	$6.2 million
Total, including others	$280 million

Principal imports (1988, excluding Colón Free Zone imports)
Mineral products	$148.2 million
Chemical and related products	$115.1 million
Machinery	$107.0 million
Total, including others	$795.5 million

Sources
International Financial Statistics, August 1990, IMF
Tom Barry, *Panama: A Country Guide*
World Development Report 1989, World Bank
Economist Intelligence Unit

Acronyms

ADO	*Alianza Democrática de Oposición*
	Democratic Opposition Alliance
ADOC	*Alianza Democrática de Oposición Cívica*
	Democratic Alliance of Civic Opposition
CAT	*Central Auténtico de Trabajadores*
	Authentic Workers' Central
CATI	*Central Auténtico de Trabajadores Independientes*
	Authentic Independent Workers' Central
CBI	Caribbean Basin Initiative
CCN	*Cruzada Civilista Nacional*
	National Civic Crusade
CEASPA	*Centro de Estudios y Acción Social Panameño*
	Panamanian Centre for Research and Social Action
CIA	Central Intelligence Agency
CIDH	*Comisión Interamericana de Derechos Humanos*
	Inter-American Human Rights Commission
CIT	*Central Istmeña de Trabajadores*
	Isthmian Workers' Central
CNT	*Confederación Nacional de Trabajadores*
	National Confederation of Workers
COLINA	*Coalición de Liberación Nacional*
	National Liberation Coalition
CONADEHUPA	*Comisión Nacional de Derechos Humanos en Panamá*
	National Commission for Human Rights in Panama
CONATO	*Consejo Nacional de Trabajadores Organizados*
	National Council of Organised Workers
CONEP	*Consejo Nacional de la Empresa Privada*
	National Council of Private Enterprise
CTRP	*Confederación de Trabajadores de la República de Panamá*
	Confederation of Workers of the Republic of Panama
DEA	Drug Enforcement Administration
DEPAT	*Dirección Ejecutiva para Asuntos del Tratado*
	Executive Directorate for Treaty Affairs
FDP	*Fuerzas de Defensa de Panamá*
	Panama Defence Forces
FENASEP	*Federación Nacional de Sindicatos de Empleados Públicos*
	National Federation of Unions of Public Employees
FP	*Fuerza Pública*
	Public Force
GN	*Guardia Nacional*
	National Guard

GSP	Generalised System of Preferences
MOLIRENA	*Movimiento Liberal Republicano Nacionalista*
	Nationalist Republican Liberal Movement
OAS	Organization of American States
PDC	*Partido Democracia Cristiana*
	Christian Democrat Party
PL	*Partido Laborista*
	Labour Party
PLA	*Partido Liberal Auténtico*
	Authentic Liberal Party
PPP	*Partido del Pueblo de Panamá*
	People's Party of Panama
PPA	*Partido Panameñista Auténtico*
	Authentic *Panameñista* Party
PR	*Partido Republicano*
	Republican Party
PRD	*Partido Revolucionario Democrático*
	Democratic Revolutionary Party
PRI	*Partido Revolucionario Institucional (Mexico)*
	Institutional Revolutionary Party (Mexico)
SELA	*Sistema Económico para América Latina*
	Latin American Economic System
SIP	*Sindicato de Industriales de Panamá*
	Panamanian Union of Industrialists
SIP	*Sociedad Interamericana de Prensa*
	Inter-American Press Society
Southcom	US Southern Command
SPP	*Sindicato de Periodistas de Panamá*
	Journalists' Union of Panama
UGT	*Unión General de Trabajadores*
	General Union of Workers
UNADE	*Unión Nacional Democrática*
	Nacional Democratic Union

Principal Political Parties and Groupings

Authentic *Panameñista* Party *(Partido Panameñista Auténtico/PPA)*

The successor to the *Panameñista* Party of Arnulfo Arias Madrid who in 1939 had declared his political platform to be 'our Panamanianism', an essentially anti-communist, populist doctrine. After having almost won the 1964 election on its own, in 1968 the PP formed part of a coalition behind Arias' presidential campaign. His presidency lasted 11 days and ended in a coup. In 1980 the party split, and the dissident wing led by Alonzo Pinzón and Luis Suárez registered for the 1980 legislative election as the PPP. By 1984, however, Arias had re-formed his party as the PPA which joined MOLIRENA and the PDC in the Democratic Opposition Alliance, backing Arias against Ardito Barletta. After Arias' death in 1988, the PPA itself split in two. One faction favoured co-operation with the military while the other joined the opposition coalition of 1989 with its leader Guillermo Endara as presidential candidate.

Christian Democrat Party *(Partido Democracia Cristiana/PDC)*

Founded in 1960, the PDC emerged out of a movement at the National University inspired by European Christian Democracy. Its leading figures were middle-class professionals, intellectuals and students, but support also came from the FTC (Federation of Christian Workers). In 1968 the radical wing of the leadership was expelled, as the party shifted to the right in support of the short-lived populist government of Arnulfo Arias. It reorganised in 1978 and came second in the 1980 election with 20 per cent of the vote, winning two seats in Congress. The PDC play a leading role in the ADOC, and is the most powerful and best organised post-invasion party.

Democratic Alliance of Civic Opposition *(Alianza Democrática de Oposición Cívica/ADOC)*

A coalition of right-wing parties founded (as the Democratic Opposition Alliance/ADO) to fight the 1984 Panamanian election, in which it won 27 seats out of 67. The PDC, PPA and MOLIRENA, which made up ADO, supported the candidacy of Arias who 'lost' the fraudulent election by 2,000 votes. In July 1987, after Díaz Herrera's revelations of Noriega's wrongdoing, ADO called for his removal. It backed the formation of the National Civic Crusade (CCN) which sought to 'demilitarise' the government. Renamed ADOC, it put forward Guillermo Endara (after much dispute) as the candidate for the May 1989 election, which he won by a substantial majority. The election results were, however, annulled. ADOC was installed as the government during the 1989 US invasion.

Democratic Revolutionary Party *(Partido Revolucionario Democrático/PRD)*

General Omar Torrijos founded the PRD in 1979 as a means to promote his political philosophy. It was closely associated with the politics of the Defence Forces, and drew its support both from poor sectors loyal to Torrijos' populism and from the wealthy who had benefited from a corrupt military regime. After Torrijos' death it moved to the right under Manuel Noriega's influence. In 1984 its candidate, Nicolás Ardito Barletta, won fraudulent elections, but was ousted by the military in September 1985 and replaced by Erick Arturo Delvalle of the Republican Party.

Labour Party *(Partido Laborista/PL)*

Formed in 1988 by Azael Vargas and Carlos Eleta, with support among elements of the army and the business sector. Despite its name and its use of a spade *(pala)* as its symbol, it is extremely conservative and hostile to organised labour. In 1984 it joined the UNADE coalition behind Ardito Barletta and obtained 3 seats in his cabinet. It was weakened by a power struggle involving the Defence Forces in 1987, but took part in the COLINA coalition.

National Civic Crusade *(Cruzada Civilista Nacional/CCN)*

Formed in June 1987 and centred on the Panamanian Chamber of Commerce, the CCN called for the resignation of Noriega and the restoration of civilian rule. Its tactics included strikes, demonstrations and 'masses for peace'. The leaders of the CCN were right-wing businessmen and the movement failed to mobilise mass support prior to the 1989 election. It had the support of the ADO parties, but not of the major labour unions.

National Liberation Coalition *(Coalición de Liberación Nacional/ COLINA)*

An alliance of 7 pro-government parties formed to succeed the UNADE alliance which won the 1984 election. UNADE was made up of the PRD, the Broad Popular Front (FRAMPO), PALA, the Liberal Party, the *Panameñista* Party and the PR. Its leading figures, Nicolás Ardito Barletta, Erick Arturo Delvalle and Roderick Esquivel, were conservative and pro-business. The new grouping (COLINA) formed to fight the 1989 election tried to distance itself from these more conservative elements. It included the PRD, PALA, PR, the Revolutionary *Panameñista* Party (PPR), the PPP and the Democratic Workers Party. The official result gave COLINA's candidate a 2:1 victory over ADOC's Endara. However, most observers agreed that Endara had won by about 3:1.

Nationalist Republican Liberal Movement *(Movimiento Liberal Republicano Nacionalista/MOLIRENA)*

Founded in 1981 chiefly from factions of the Liberal and Republican parties, MOLIRENA joined the ADO coalition for the 1984 election and later supported the CCN campaign to remove the military from politics. In 1989 MOLIRENA leader Guillermo Ford became vice-president of the re-named ADOC. After the US invasion he was appointed the Second Vice-President and Minister of Planning. MOLIRENA was allocated 15 Assembly seats by the electoral tribunal.

People's Party of Panama *(Partido del Pueblo de Panamá/PPP)*

Founded in 1925 as the Labour Party, the PPP took its present name in 1943 having previously been known as the Communist Party. As Panama's pro-Soviet communist party, it was successful during the 1940's in organising a broad popular and labour movement. After the 1968 coup it was at first repressed by Torrijos, but by 1970 it was incorporated into Torrijos' nationalist and populist alliance, in which it took a leading role. In 1989 it formed part of the COLINA alliance.

Republican Party *(Partido Republicano/PR)*

Founded in 1960 by J D Bazán and Max and Erick Arturo Delvalle, all of them Jewish. Bazán was briefly vice-president to Arias in 1968 despite the latter's anti-semitism. Closely allied to the country's elite, the PR joined the UNADE coalition behind Ardito Barletta in 1984, winning two seats. After Ardito Barletta's overthrow by the military in 1985, Delvalle became Panama's president, but following his attempt to dismiss Noriega, Delvalle himself was removed in February 1988. The PR joined the COLINA coalition for the 1989 election.

Chronology

1821	Panama declares independence from Spain and becomes a province of Gran Colombia.
1903	Secessionists declare the department of Panama an independent republic; the new flag is raised by a member of the United States Army Corps of Engineers as US gunboats prevent the landing of Colombian troops. US Secretary of State John Hay and French entrepreneur Philippe Bunau-Varilla formulate a canal treaty very favourable to the US.
1904	US troops intervene to quash protest against the Hay-Bunau-Varilla Treaty. New constitution promulgated which grants the US the right to intervene 'in any part of Panama to re-establish public peace and constitutional order.' National army disbanded. Panama establishes monetary system based on the US dollar.
1914	Panama Canal begins operation.
1936	Panama and the US sign the General Treaty of Friendship and Cooperation, which maintains most stipulations of 1903 treaty except the guarantee of Panama's independence and Washington's right to intervene in Panama.
1939	Revised treaty ratified by US Senate.
1940	National Party candidate Arnulfo Arias Madrid elected.
1941	New constitution promulgated. Adolfo de la Guardia replaces Arias in a coup.
1942	New six-year treaty with the US allows US bases and airfields on Panamanian territory. Many US military bases built after US entry into World War II.
1946	New constitution promulgated; Enrique Jiménez elected as provisional president. US army opens the School of the Americas in violation of the 1903 treaty which allows US troops only for the defence of the canal.
1947	National Assembly rejects new treaty on US military bases, after public protests.
1949	Death of President Díaz Arosemena; succession by First

Vice-President Daniel Chanis, who attempts to dismiss National Guard Commander José Antonio Remón Cantera, but is ousted himself. Remón installs Arias.

1951   Arias ousted; formation of a coalition government led by Alcibiades Arosemena.

1953   US creates the Panamanian National Guard, modelled on Anastasio Somoza's Nicaraguan National Guard.

1956   Treaty of Mutual Understanding and Cooperation (Remón-Eisenhower Treaty) signed.

1962   Presidents Chiari and Kennedy agree to name negotiators to review the 1903 treaty; also agree to display the Panamanian flag in the Canal Zone.

1964
January   Canal Zone residents attack students attempting to fly the Panamanian flag next to the US flag at a high school. During subsequent flag riots more than 20 people are killed, more than 300 wounded, and over 500 arrested; Panama severs diplomatic relations with US; OAS called in to mediate.

April   Diplomatic relations with the US restored; negotiations begin to draft new treaties to resolve the conflicts.

1968   Constitutional crisis; Arnulfo Arias Madrid elected again but deposed after 11 days. Junta is formed, but power is assumed by Colonel Omar Torrijos Herrera after he overthrows coup leader Boris Martínez.

1969   Abortive coup attempt against Torrijos; with the aid of Manuel Noriega he survives and consolidates power.

1972   New constitution promulgated; Torrijos named 'Supreme Leader of the Panamanian Revolution' with virtually unlimited powers.

New Labour Code becomes effective

1973   United Nations Security Council meets in Panama and exhorts Panama and the US to continue negotiations for a treaty returning the Canal Zone to Panama. The US vetoes the resolution.

1974   Panama and the US agree to begin new negotiations.

1976   New Labour Law negates many of the benefits of the 1972 Code.

1977   Presidents Torrijos and Carter sign the Panama Canal

Treaties in Washington DC giving Panama control of the canal at noon on 31 December 1999. The accords replace the US-run Panama Canal Company with a jointly supervised Panama Canal Commission. A Panamanian to take office as administrator of the Commission on 1 January 1990. Panamanian National Assembly approves the Canal Treaties.

1978	Canal Treaties ratified by US Senate with a provision that permits US intervention if the canal's operation is interrupted, though such action shall not be interpreted as a right of intervention in Panama's sovereignty or internal affairs.
	National Assembly elects Aristides Royo president.
	Formation of Democratic Revolutionary Party (PRD).
1979	Panama Canal Treaties go into effect and Canal Zone officially ceases to exist.
1981	Torrijos dies in an unexplained plane crash; Colonel Florencio Flórez succeeds him as head of the National Guard.
1982	President Royo resigns under pressure from National Guard; Ricardo de la Espriella becomes President.
	Rubén Darío Paredes ousts Flórez as head of the National Guard.
1983	National Guard reorganised and named Panama Defence Forces (FDP); Paredes resigns.
July 31	General Manuel Antonio Noriega, head of military intelligence and a CIA asset trained at the School of the Americas, becomes commander of the Panama Defence Forces.
1984 February	President de la Espriella resigns and is replaced by Jorge Illueca.
May	PRD candidate Nicolás Ardito Barletta narrowly defeats Arnulfo Arias Madrid in fraudulent elections.
September	School of the Americas closes after training 45,000 Latin American officers; it relocates in Fort Benning, Georgia, four months later.
October 11	Ardito Barletta is sworn in as President. Secretary of State George Shultz attends the inauguration ceremony and calls him 'a long-time and respected friend'.

1985
September

Dr Hugo Spadafora, former vice-minister of health, is assassinated upon his return from a visit to Costa Rica. The military is accused of complicity in his assassination; Ardito Barletta resigns; Noriega installs Vice-President Erick Arturo Delvalle.

1987
June 1

FDP general staff announces the retirement of FDP second-in-command Colonel Roberto Díaz Herrera, after more than 25 years of service.

June 7

Díaz Herrera accuses Noriega of rigging the 1984 election and murdering Dr Spadafora; anti-government rioting breaks out; ten-day 'state of emergency' declared; constitutional guarantees suspended.

June 26

US Senate approves a resolution calling for Noriega to step down, an independent investigation of corruption charges against senior officers and new elections.

A hundred protestors attack US Embassy; US demands payment for damages to building.

July 1

OAS approves resolution calling on the US to stop interfering in Panama's internal affairs.

August

US Secretary of State George Shultz announces that Washington has suspended aid to Panama ($3 million for FY88).

1988
February 5

US attorneys in Florida announce Noriega's indictment on drug-trafficking charges. February President Delvalle attempts to fire Noriega, but is himself ousted by the National Assembly, and replaced by Manuel Solís Palma. Delvalle goes into hiding but is recognised by the US as Panama's president.

Run begins on national banks by depositors, and opposition organises strikes.

March

US government freezes Panama's assets abroad and Delvalle urges a boycott of the country.

Government closes the nation's banks for nine weeks.

US government suspends Panama Canal Commission's payments to the Panamanian government.

Coup attempt fails; massive power shortages shut down trans-isthmian oil pipeline; transportation disrupted; two week general strike.

Noriega forms Dignity Battalions to fight against a possible US invasion.

April 8 US President Ronald Reagan invokes the Emergency Powers Act of 1977 to bar US companies and individuals from making any payments to the Panamanian government. Instead he asks them to make payments to the Delvalle-controlled Federal Reserve account.

May Secret bargaining collapses between Reagan administration and Noriega.

July CIA develops a coup plan that might result in Noriega's assassination by dissident officers; plan blocked by Senate Select Committee on Intelligence.

1989
May ADOC candidate Guillermo Endara wins presidential election; election nullified by Noriega regime.

President Bush recalls US ambassador and dispatches an additional 2,000 troops to Panama; Pentagon stages a series of aggressive manoeuvres.

OAS forms mediation commission comprising foreign ministers of Ecuador, Guatemala, and Trinidad & Tobago.

July OAS ministers propose that Noriega step down, a government of transition take power, and elections be held at a later date; they also call for an end to US military and economic aggression, compliance with 1977 Canal Treaties, and OAS mediation during the negotiating process.

The US commander in Panama, critical of Washington's escalatory policies, is replaced by General Maxwell R Thurman who begins to prepare for an invasion.

August Panama calls for an urgent meeting of the UN Security Council in response to US manoeuvres.

September General Council of State names provisional government led by Francisco Rodríguez and announces elections will be called within six months after sanctions are lifted. US withdraws its ambassador; many Latin American ambassadors recalled for consultations.

October 3 Failed coup attempt against Noriega.

November Bush administration announces ban on Panamanian-flagged ships using US ports.

December	Noriega's *ad hoc* Assembly appoints him head of state with unlimited powers.
	US invades with 26,000 troops and installs Endara as President.
1990	
January 3	Noriega surrenders to US forces. Colonel Roberto Armijo resigns as head of FP; replaced by Colonel Eduardo Herrera.
January 4	Noriega arraigned in Miami on drug charges.
January 10	US and Panama sign general drugs accord.
January 25	President Bush promises $1 billion aid.
February 7	US Congress authorises $42 million humanitarian aid.
February 12	FDP formally abolished and replaced by Public Force.
February 13	Pentagon says all invasion troops withdrawn.
March 2	US soldier dies in grenade attack on bar. Endara begins two-week fast in solidarity with the people of Panama.
March 23	Cuban ambassador to Panama expelled.
April 4	Panama rejects Group of Eight call for election.
May 25	US Congress approves $420 million aid to Panama.
June 20	8,000 demonstrators call for compensation for losses caused by the invasion.
August 13	Government-appointed Reconciliation Commission demands end to occupation.
August 24	FP commander Colonel Herrera resigns; replaced by Colonel Fernando Quezada.
September 4	Colonel Quezada sacked.
September 10	Largest-ever cocaine seizure in Panama — 2 tons.

Charter of the Organization of American States

Article 18:
No State or group of States has the right to intervene, directly or indirectly, for any reason whatever, in the internal or external affairs of any other State.

Article 20:
The territory of a State is inviolable; it may not be the object, even temporarily, of military occupation or of other measures of force taken by another State, directly or indirectly, on any grounds whatever.

Statement of Understanding appended to the Panama Canal Treaty (1977)

That [Panama and the US] shall ... defend the canal against any threat to the regime of neutrality ... This does not mean, nor shall it be interpreted as the right of intervention of the US in the internal affairs of Panama. US action ... shall never be directed against the territorial integrity or political independence of Panama.

Introduction
Of Rights and Wrongs

The US invasion of Panama on 20 December 1989 was a crime both in international law and against civilised values. It was also a spectacularly successful crime, bringing prestige to the perpetrator and apparently received with enthusiasm by the victim.

That the United States committed such a crime should come as little surprise: it has been a persistent offender. The 1989 invasion was its twentieth military intervention on the isthmus of Panama, leaving aside innumerable similar offences elsewhere in the region.

Strong nations commonly make great efforts to convince domestic and foreign public opinion of the virtue and purity of their intentions when committing outrages against weaker ones. Rarely has any been so successful in such a propaganda effort as the Reagan-Bush administration. Dominant groups in US society have viewed Panama as a suitable case for intervention virtually since its independence from Spain, and on this occasion, not for the first time, the US public seems overwhelmingly to have endorsed this view.

Equally important was the initial enthusiasm of a majority of the Panamanian population for what one former US ambassador to Panama termed the 'blitzkrieg' unleashed on the country. Great powers invariably contend that local populations welcome their invasions as they would a divine deliverance; in Panama it seemed to be true. This was the ultimate justification of the crime: if the victim did not object, by what right did anyone else?

The invasion of Panama, however, raises fundamental and disturbing issues for those who seek a more just and equitable world order. Illegal as it was, the military action of the government of the US removed from power an unsavoury dictator who enjoyed little support in his own land. When the invasion came, most Panamanians treated those who resisted as criminals, and the invaders as liberators.

Ultimately, of course, it is for Panamanians to decide what role, if any, they wish the US to play in their domestic politics. Even as they celebrated Noriega's departure, many recalled that he owed his power, as well as his downfall, to the US government. The invaders' popularity began to fade as the limited extent of Washington's commitment to restoring what its policies had damaged and destroyed became apparent. The government it had installed no longer represented the only alternative to Noriega; it had to stand or fall on its own abilities, and these soon began to be questioned, along with the continuing US presence.

However, it is for the world as a whole to decide whether one nation should be allowed to determine how another is governed. In July 1990, seven months after the invasion of Panama, a US State Department official pronounced the following dictum:

> '[T]here is no place for coercion and intimidation in a civilised world. All disputes should be settled by peaceful means.'

Within days, the US was leading a worldwide campaign of economic sanctions against Saddam Hussein's Iraq, which had unilaterally invaded its smaller neighbour, Kuwait. As in Panama, the aggressor claimed to be acting in the interests of its neighbour's people. As in Panama, the underlying reasons related to the strategic interests of the aggressor. It is not necessary to suggest an exact parallel between the US invasion of Panama and the Iraqi invasion of Kuwait to see the double standard applied not only in Washington but by US allies.

The US had also played its part in creating and arming Saddam Hussein, only the latest in a seemingly endless line of foreign dictators whose continuance in power it deemed preferable to the perceived alternatives. In the post-Cold War world there may at last be a chance to turn democracy, self-determination and respect for human rights into standards by which every nation is judged. Where these are violated, concerted international action may at last begin to be effective. But if the strongest military power on earth continues to play by different rules, asserting its right to act alone, the chances for a new and better world order will be greatly reduced.

Chapter I
Operation 'Just Cause'

The twentieth US military intervention in Panama began slightly ahead of schedule, at half-past-midnight on 20 December 1989. Thirty minutes before 'H-hour' the 6th Mechanised Battalion of the US Army's 5th Division, supported by four Sheridan light tanks, began its advance on the Panama Defence Forces (*Fuerzas de Defensa de Panamá* — FDP) headquarters, the *Comandancia*. Word of the invasion had leaked out, and the head of the Panama-based US Southern Command (Southcom), General Max Thurman, was anxious to move fast.

Task Force Bayonet, of which the tanks and armoured personnel carriers were part, was charged with decapitating the FDP. Two assault companies, helicoptered in from Howard Air Force Base just across the Panama Canal, blocked off support from nearby Fort Amador. An infantry battalion and helicopter gunships were also involved in the main assault. The troops knew their target. Most had been in Panama since the abortive election seven months earlier and they were hardly likely to lose their way.

The invasion relied on overwhelming force. In addition to over 13,000 troops already stationed at US bases in Panama, Washington ordered in a further 7,000, including Rangers, Marines, Special Forces and the 82nd Airborne (veterans of the 1983 Grenada invasion). Subsequent reinforcements brought the total to over 26,000. In all, it was the most extensive US military operation since the Vietnam war, and involved the biggest combat paratroop drop (4,500) since the Allied attempt to seize the Rhine bridges in 1944.

The airborne troops, flying in from six US bases, had the job of preventing the FDP's elite units — Battalion 2000 and the *Machos de Monte* — from reinforcing the Panama City garrison. They also had to seize key points such as the Omar Torrijos international airport and vulnerable installations like the Sierra Tigre power station and the

Madden Dam (whose reservoir supplies the water for the Panama Canal), and release some 50 prisoners whose lives might otherwise have been threatened.

It was scarcely surprising that the FDP knew something was about to happen. Throughout the previous day, military cargo aircraft had been landing at Howard, bringing supplies and equipment for the invasion. Moreover (according to *Newsweek* magazine), there had been at least a dozen security leaks, and rumours were spreading.

As the invasion began, a foreign journalist who had been hoping for a quiet Christmas was on the phone in the lobby of the Hotel Ejecutivo, trying to convince an editor in London that rumours of an invasion were exaggerated. At that moment the first bombs dropped.

The seismological station at the University of Panama registered 417 explosions over the following 14 hours — one bomb every two minutes. Compared to the bombings of Hanoi and other Vietnamese cities in the early 1970s, this rain of destruction was relatively benign — considerably less than the payload of one of the B52s that plied the long route from Guam in the South Pacific to the crowded cities of Indochina.

Even so, the 417 explosions that night brought death and misery to the poorer quarters of Panama City, clustered around military installations the invaders had to take at all costs. Around 15,000 Panamanians celebrated Christmas Day in makeshift accommodation after their homes had been destroyed.

For the residents of the exclusive Punta Paitilla district, in their high-rise apartments across the bay from the *Comandancia*, the rockets, bombs and tracer bullets were little more dangerous than a spectacular firework display. Some sat in their living rooms with a panoramic view of the action — glass in hand to toast the downfall of the military regime many of them detested.

Due care was taken not to disturb them unnecessarily. Just down the road lay Paitilla airport, where the most wanted man in Panama at that moment — FDP commander General Manuel Noriega — kept his personal jet. US Southcom assigned this target to the US Navy's elite SEAL commandos, who were ordered to disable the plane at close quarters in order to avoid 'collateral damage' from stray rounds to diplomatic residences in the vicinity. This high-risk option cost the lives of four SEALs.

No such concern for civilians, however, governed operations in El Chorrillo district, the slum area immediately around the *Comandancia*. In order to minimise US casualties, the FDP headquarters 'was shelled from at least two directions for about four hours before US troops approached it at dawn,' according to a report by the human rights

A US armoured personnel carrier patrols Panama's city centre, three days after the invasion.   (Popperfoto)

organisation Americas Watch. Not surprisingly, this took a heavy toll in civilian lives.

Southcom gave no warning to the civilian population until US ground troops entered the area, when they used loudspeakers to order residents to evacuate. Earlier, while the shelling was continuing, US helicopters had broadcast surrender calls to the FDP troops. Southcom told Americas Watch that there was no overriding military requirement that would have prevented the same system being used to provide a warning to civilians (and thereby to save lives) — yet none was given.

With some exceptions — such as the Paitilla airport operation — Southcom strategy was to avoid US casualties. A university professor who watched the assault on the Gamboa military police barracks noted that the US troops 'didn't want [to sustain] casualties and they were taking great care of themselves'. Made of wood, the barracks offered no protection to the defenders. 'So the Americans shouted to them to surrender ... I saw three soldiers come out of the barracks and they were immediately machine-gunned, so the rest of the troops carried on shooting and didn't surrender.' 'American casualties are the ones that count,' the professor added, 'the casualties of the people can be any number but they don't count.'

How Many Died?

Estimates of the number of Panamanians who died in the invasion vary enormously, in large measure because US military commanders gave a low priority to counting the 'enemy' dead and wounded, or to determining how many of them were civilians.

In the immediate aftermath of the invasion Southcom announced that 314 FDP members had died, along with 202 civilians. These figures were immediately challenged by supporters of the defeated Noriega regime, who claimed that 6,000-7,000 had died.

Some credence was given to the opposition account by an Independent Commission of Inquiry composed of prominent US citizens including former US Attorney-General Ramsey Clark, other lawyers and clergy. The Commission concluded that 'as many as 4,000 to 7,000 people may have been killed'.

Whilst it is true that many bodies were buried in mass graves (a standard military procedure, especially in a hot climate), this was not necessarily motivated by a desire to cover up the number of fatalities. The Americas Watch delegation, while convinced that 'the effort to count the dead has been inadequate', found no evidence of 'a deliberate attempt to hide the real numbers'.

However, a delegation from the US organisation Physicians for Human Rights found the Southcom figure for military deaths to be well in excess of the number of verifiable FDP corpses, and in March 1990 the Pentagon was forced to concede that only 51 of these had been confirmed. Its original statements drew on claims from US soldiers of battlefield 'kills'.

The Pentagon did not, however, reduce its estimate for the overall death toll, which suggests that only one in ten of those Panamanians who died was a soldier (though some at least of the remainder must presumably have been Dignity Battalion members).

Both Physicians for Human Rights and Americas Watch put the figure for civilian dead at around 300. Although declaring itself open to fresh evidence, Americas Watch noted that the 'insistence on higher numbers has the unwanted effect of minimising the tragedy of the dozens of civilians who most assuredly did die'.

Americas Watch, too, condemned the double standards:

> 'At the very moment in which the attack on the (FDP) headquarters started, a Delta Force team of US troops conducted a daring commando raid on the Cárcel Modelo, Panama's central penitentiary, located just across the street from the *Comandancia*. The purpose of the raid . . . was to rescue US citizen Kurt Muse, a (CIA) operative jailed there. There was no resistance from the guards and the jail was left open so that the majority of common crime offenders escaped . . . In our view, this carefully planned and risky operation stands in contrast with the absolute lack of concern for the safety of thousands of innocent civilians in El Chorrillo.'

El Chorrillo was home to around 30,000 people, most of them living in ramshackle wooden buildings built early this century to house the labourers who built the Panama Canal. The remainder occupied a number of residential tower blocks, known as *multifamiliares*, or *multis*. Despite the lateness of the hour, many were still awake — reading, watching a tv soap opera, catching up on household chores.

A fisherman who lived in El Chorrillo's 25th Street had gone across the road to the corner shop to buy cigarettes when the bombing started:

> 'The owner of the shop shut the doors and told me to get down on the floor. For a good while I felt the heat on my back from the house next door, which was on fire. Then for a moment the shooting stopped and I was able to run out of the shop. In the street I met a friend who had been wounded and he asked me to help him. We ran and stood up against a wall, there was a burst of gunfire and when I looked round my friend had been killed. I ran, and in the streets I saw children, women, old people, dead men, and the tanks were running over their bodies. People think it was nothing what happened, but if they'd lived through what we did... It was terrible. My family lost everything.'

Southcom admitted that the fires which broke out in El Chorrillo may partly have been caused by flares and tracer bullets used by US troops. Exploding tanks of household gas set off other blazes. However, some seem to have been set deliberately, by unidentified men in plain clothes. Whatever their origin, the fires destroyed several city blocks and took a heavy toll in civilian lives.

El Chorrillo: some of the survivors search for their possessions in the wreckage of an apartment block.

(Bill Robinson/*The Observer*)

'Why have they done this to us?'

This is how the young woman who lived in one of the *multifamiliares*, the tower blocks of El Chorrillo, described her experiences on 20 December.

'I was ironing when I heard the first gunfire from the direction of [Fort] Amador. We went out onto the balcony, from where we could see red lights which the neighbours said were rockets or shells. After 30 or 40 minutes four helicopters appeared, flying towards the Central Barracks [the *Comandancia*]. They must have been firing all kinds of missiles, because we could hear shots and explosions of different intensities.

Then the lights went out over the whole *barrio* and the fires started, especially in the wooden houses nearest the barracks. It was chaos. When the fires began the people in the burning houses tried to escape towards the Avenue of the Martyrs, but they were caught between the helicopters and the tanks and armoured cars of the gringos, which were advancing along with the foot soldiers, firing as they went.

We could hardly believe it. My little boy was crying with terror, my sister and I tried to protect him with our bodies. Every time a bomb fell the building shook and windows were smashed . . . in between the explosions we could hear cries of pain and fear. After about 45 minutes we started to hear a voice from a helicopter telling the Panamanian soldiers, in Spanish, to surrender. They responded with gunfire and grenades.

The people in our building whose flats were nearest the barracks came out into the corridors. We didn't know how best to protect ourselves, because bullets kept coming into almost all the flats. At one point I dragged myself into the kitchen and struggled to get the two gas tanks into the bathroom, which I thought was the safest place. In many of the flats the gas tanks exploded when bullets hit them.

This lasted until about 2.30am, when there was a short period of calm, a little over half an hour in which we just heard isolated shots. I was able to calm my son down a little and in the dark I tried to put some clothing into a bag . . .

Then the Americans began firing again, from the helicopters and from the ground . . . Around 7am they ordered civilians to leave the area as quickly as possible "because we are going to bomb again" . . . in the streets everything was confusion and panic. On the pavements there were the bodies of civilians, men, women, children, mangled bodies, some of them burned. Many people were sobbing and saying, "My God, what has happened, why have they done this to us?"

. . . I couldn't tell you how many bodies, but a lot, not ten, not twenty, there were lots of them. And we also saw parts of bodies — a piece of leg over here, a foot over there, intestines, hands, etc. I tried not to let my little boy see, and I tried not to look myself because it made me cry and I felt sick . . . a little beyond the limit [of the former Canal Zone], close to where there was an FDP post, we saw a great trench where they had thrown a heap of bodies, I think there must have been 100 bodies piled up there.'

Report of joint mission to Panama by the Latin American Human Rights Association (ALDHU) and the Commission on US — Latin American Relations, February 1990

There was never any doubt as to who would win the battle of Panama City. On paper, the FDP's strength stood at some 16,000, but this included police and other non-military personnel. No more than 5,000 of its number could in any sense be regarded as combat troops. Many were simply traffic police or customs officers. The Panamanians had no effective military radar, anti-aircraft batteries or true air force. They were up against the world's greatest military power, using the latest technology: Apache helicopter gunships; the awesome AC-130 aircraft, equipped with everything up to howitzers and capable of firing 17,000 rounds of ammunition a minute; even the F117A 'stealth' ground-attack aircraft, whose radar-invisibility was wholly irrelevant in the circumstances and whose intervention was intended to convince a sceptical Congress to fund its production.

The stealth aircraft dropped their 2,000lb bombs with what US Defense Secretary Dick Cheney described as 'pinpoint accuracy'. However, he later admitted under pressure that at least one of the bombs landed so far from the target that Southcom had to mount a search to find the point of impact.

Most FDP units surrendered fairly quickly, but with General Noriega on the run it took US troops several days to bring the military situation under a semblance of control. Panamanian soldiers who had shed their uniforms continued to put up resistance, along with members of the paramilitary Dignity Battalions, created by Noriega in 1988.

The failure to capture Noriega immediately was only one of the flaws in an operation which its planner, General Carl Stiner, hailed as so successful that 'there were no lessons learned.' As in Grenada, many of the US casualties (perhaps up to 60 per cent) were self-inflicted. Nine of the 23 US soldiers killed died as a result of 'friendly fire'.

Spanish news photographer Juantxu Rodríguez died in just such an incident, outside the Marriott Hotel. He was caught in crossfire when two different US units apparently mistook each other for Panamanians. The New York-based Committee for the Protection of Journalists judged the US government's response to its questions about this incident 'unsatisfactory'. However Washington denied any obligation to compensate Rodríguez' family, who have sued the Pentagon for a million dollars.

In the aftermath of the invasion, after having destroyed the FDP as a police force as well as an army, the US military authorities made no attempt to fill the policing vacuum. The result was an orgy of looting in Panama City and Colón, organised in some cases by the Dignity Battalions, which caused losses calculated at $1.2 billion. US Assistant Secretary of State Lawrence Eagleburger, who arrived in early January at the head of a group of senior Bush administration officials, dismissed suggestions of US responsibility for the destruction. Insurance companies, meanwhile, claimed that losses from looting fell under their war exclusion clauses, exempting them from the need to pay compensation. Over 60 companies, including US subsidiaries, subsequently filed a lawsuit against the US government for damages.

For these glorious feats of arms the Pentagon was reported to have ordered 44,000 Combat Infantryman Badges, even though only 2,500 of its troops actually engaged in combat. The handful of women

US soldier gives belated protection to one of the few supermarkets to escape looting. (Bill Robinson/*The Observer*)

honoured are in any case not entitled to their medals, since regulations forbid their going into combat at all.

The Department of Defense claimed that some of the badges will be used for extra uniforms and souvenirs (which must explain why the medals outnumber the total troops involved by almost two to one). But some idea of the rigorous criteria applied can be gleaned from the 18 Purple Hearts (awarded to those wounded in action) that have been requested for paratroopers who broke or sprained their ankles when landing. This cavalier approach to military honours followed the precedent set by the invasion of Grenada in 1983, when the 20,000 troops involved were awarded 28,802 medals.

Selective Chivalry

The official code name for the invasion was Operation Just Cause, picked at the last minute by Defense Secretary Dick Cheney to replace the random computer designation 'Blue Spoon'. The name has a defensive air about it, suggesting that Washington anticipated that world opinion would overwhelming reject its unilateral military action.

Senior government figures, including Cheney and President Bush himself, had gone on record as rejecting the military option following the failed coup attempt of 3 October. Bush had said military intervention was 'not prudent, and that's not the way I plan to conduct the military or foreign affairs of this country.' Explaining the sudden U-turn, Cheney said:

> 'I think we as a government bent over backward to avoid having to take military action. I think the record is replete with the patience and forbearance of the US government in this instance. When it reached the point, however, when it was clear that American lives were at risk, when it reached the point where it was clear that General Noriega had created an environment in which his troops felt free to terrorise and brutalise Americans who had every legitimate and lawful right to be in Panama, that was a fundamentally different set of circumstances.'

Bush himself set out these circumstances in more detail in his address to the nation on the morning of 20 December:

> 'Last Friday, Noriega declared his military dictatorship to be in a state of war with the US, and publicly threatened the lives of Americans in Panama. The very next day, forces under his command shot and killed an unarmed American serviceman, wounded another, arrested and brutally beat a third American serviceman, and then brutally interrogated his wife, threatening her with sexual abuse. That was enough.'

But was it? The circumstances leading up to the invasion provide no moral or legal justification for the overthrow of a foreign government, the killing of hundreds of unarmed civilians and the removal for trial in the US of the head of state of a country whose constitution forbids the extradition of its citizens.

Bush gave four main reasons for his action:
● to safeguard the lives of US citizens
● to defend democracy in Panama
● to combat drug trafficking [primarily by apprehending Manuel Noriega and bringing him to trial in the US], and
● to 'protect the integrity' of the 1977 Panama Canal Treaties.

With regard to American lives, Southcom had at its disposal in Panama 13,000 troops who were better armed, trained and co-ordinated than the FDP. This force was more than adequate to protect US civilians. Further, protecting US lives did not require an attack on the old city of Panama, nor pitched battles in working-class *barrios*. If anything, the invasion endangered US civilians (not to mention US soldiers) by leaving them vulnerable to hostage-taking. One hostage was indeed killed — Ray Dragseth, a professor of computer science at the Panama Canal College, who was taken from his apartment by armed men just after the invasion.

As Alexander Cockburn pointed out in the magazine *New Statesman & Society* (12 January 1990), concerning the President's outrage at the treatment of the US officer's wife, 'Bush's chivalry is sparingly dispensed'. Cockburn contrasted the invasion of Panama with US inaction over the kidnap and torture only a month earlier of a US nun, Sister Diana Ortíz, by Guatemalans apparently operating with police protection. The State Department justified its failure to act by saying that the matter came under Guatemalan jurisdiction.

Nor does the argument that the invasion was needed to 'defend democracy' withstand scrutiny. Late in the evening of 19 December, Southcom summoned the leaders of the civilian opposition, Guillermo Endara, Ricardo Arias Calderón and Guillermo Ford to a US military base, Fort Clayton. At around 2am they were sworn in as President and First and Second Vice-Presidents respectively, in a ceremony witnessed by two leaders of the Panamanian Human Rights Committee. Fort Clayton remained the seat of the new government for about 30 hours, before Endara's provisional headquarters was moved to the Legislative Assembly building.

One of the five Panamanians present at the dubious investiture, speaking anonymously to the *Miami Herald,* said, 'we were taken to Fort Clayton at about midnight, and told we couldn't make outside phone calls or leave the room. The ceremony took place at about 2am, and we agreed to say it had taken place in Panamanian territory.'

Observers of the May 1989 election, in which Endara, Arias and Ford headed the opposition ADOC coalition, had concluded that the opposition had won an overwhelming victory. The Noriega regime had annulled the results because its own COLINA alliance, headed by Carlos Duque, had fared so badly that even massive fraud could not hide the true result. In this sense, the ADOC leaders were undoubtedly more entitled to form a government than the regime they replaced. But the circumstances of their coming to power seriously undermined their legitimacy. Endara himself admitted that they had not even been consulted about the invasion, merely 'informed'. He added that it had been 'like a kick in the head' and that he 'would have been happier without it'.

Moreover, the US commitment to Panamanian democracy was itself a very recent phenomenon. When the Noriega regime rigged the 1984 election to ensure a victory for the official candidate, Nicolás Ardito

Barletta, the US embassy soon had clear and detailed evidence of the fraud. It chose, however, to place its own interests above those of the Panamanians, preferring the fraudulently elected — but dependable — Ardito Barletta over the true victor, the veteran populist Arnulfo Arias. Arias, long regarded as hostile to the US, received little sympathy as US Secretary of State George Shultz attended the inauguration, praising 'Panamanian democracy'.

In 1985 Noriega ousted Barletta and replaced him with his (equally fraudulently elected) vice-president, Erick Arturo Delvalle. But when, in February 1988, Delvalle tried to sack General Noriega, and was himself removed from office, Washington chose to continue treating him as the legitimate president of Panama.

The US public, which gave the invasion an 80-90 per cent approval rating, found the drug trafficking argument the most persuasive. The evidence of Noriega's involvement with narcotics is examined in Chapter Three, but it is worth noting here that the decision by the US Justice Department in 1988 not to block the indictment of the general on drugs charges was at least as much a political as a judicial choice. Washington had blocked earlier attempts on grounds of 'national security', but by this stage it was clear that the former ally could not be saved.

The US government had known of Noriega's involvement with drug trafficking since the early 1970s. The right signals from Washington at an earlier stage would probably have limited, if not altogether halted this aspect of his activities. There have been other cases involving leading foreign politicians or military personnel, in the Bahamas and Honduras for example, in which the US has also discouraged the pursuit of investigations and indictments for 'reasons of state'.

Using the Canal Treaties to justify the invasion is equally dubious. Under the 1977 Carter-Torrijos Treaties the US retains the right to defend the canal against any threat to its neutrality, even beyond the handover in the year 2000. However, to ensure that the right of intervention in Panama enshrined in the 1903 treaty would not be carried forward, the then Panamanian leader, General Torrijos, refused to reach an accord until wording was included which unambiguously prohibited the US from meddling in the political affairs of Panama.

According to the Statement of Understanding appended to the treaties, the reference to canal neutrality 'does not mean, nor shall it be interpreted as the right of intervention of the US in the internal affairs of Panama. US action ... shall never be directed against the territorial integrity or political independence of Panama.' Far from being a fulfilment of its treaty obligations, the US invasion blatantly violated the Canal Treaties. It also closed the canal for the first time since it opened in 1914 (other than once as a result of a landslide). Washington never presented any evidence to show that a threat to the canal existed prior to the invasion.

Last Straws

Both Bush and Cheney cited the Panamanian 'declaration of war' and the attacks on US military personnel in their speeches justifying the invasion.

Soon after the invasion, it became clear that these incidents, together with Noriega's assumption of the formal status of head of state, did not so much provoke as accelerate the invasion plan, which was already at an advanced stage. The notion that a military operation involving upwards of 20,000 troops could be planned and set in motion in 72 hours is, in any case, manifestly absurd.

According to one retired US military source, with a high security clearance, Southcom set the invasion for 1 January 1990, but then brought it forward in response to the events of 15-16 December.

On Friday 15 December the 510-member, *ad hoc* National Assembly of Representatives (*Asamblea Nacional de Corregimientos*), a rubber-stamp 'parliament' revived by Noriega to give his regime some semblance of legitimacy, appointed him head of state. A formal resolution stated that the move was necessary because 'the Republic of Panama is in a state of war while there is aggression against the people of Panama from the United States of America.'

For over two years the Reagan-Bush administration had publicly campaigned to remove from office the *de facto* head of the Panamanian government. For 18 months, Washington had subjected Panama to a barrage of economic sanctions, propaganda broadcasts from Southcom bases and displays of heavily-armed troops in the streets of Panama City. Given Washington's repeated refusal to rule out military intervention, these troop movements could hardly be viewed as innocent — indeed, US officials made it clear that the purpose of sending the troops forth on their unspecified errands was precisely to raise the level of tension. Further, the US Congress had approved a widely publicised 'covert' aid package to finance the overthrow of the Noriega regime.

Had Panama truly been delcaring war, it would in any case have been a declaration without content. Lacking both an airforce and a navy, and with a population 100 times smaller than that of the US, Panama presented no credible threat. Had Panama declared war on the US and then deliberately set out to kill US servicemen, a case might have been made for limited US military action in 'self-defence' under Article 51 of the UN Charter. However, this was not what happened.

Just after 9pm on the night of Saturday 16 December, a group of four US marines in a civilian vehicle ran an FDP roadblock near the *Comandancia*. They appear to have taken a wrong turning, and then a wrong decision. One of the bullets fired after them as they headed towards the FDP headquarters killed First Lieutenant Robert Paz, 24, who was sitting in the back seat of the car. The FDP troops then made matters worse by seizing a navy lieutenant and his wife and subjecting them to a brutal interrogation.

In the atmosphere of tension to which both sides had contributed, the only surprising thing is that this was the first fatality. No amount of intelligence data suggesting that Noriega himself was becoming 'unstable' can support the conclusion that the regime sought to commit suicide by provoking an all-out military confrontation with the US. Lieutenant Paz's death was a tragic mistake, arising out of jumpiness on both sides. But for Washington, it provided the ideal pretext for an invasion.

A former Pentagon spokesman, Fred Hoffman, who had access to the planning documents, contradicted the US official line when he told *Newsweek*, 'they had a plan and they were just waiting for an excuse to use it.' General Fred Woerner, replaced as head of Southcom by General Max Thurman three months earlier, claimed that he was removed over his reluctance to support an invasion. Thurman (known to his subordinates as 'Mad Max') had no such qualms; nor indeed did his deputy, army commander General Mark Cisneros, who has since said that it was a pity Fidel Castro did not intervene in defence of Noriega, because that way the US could have finished him off as well.

A failed coup attempt on 3 October 1989 was the watershed. US troops blocked some streets in support of the rebels but did not otherwise intervene, and the US Congress heavily criticised their restraint, reviving the 'wimp' accusation that Bush was trying to shake off. The opinion polls showed that a majority of US voters favoured military action; the first time since the Vietnam War that the prospect of an overseas conflict had commanded such support.

Anxious to bury the 'Vietnam syndrome' once and for all, rightwing ideologues like Elliott Abrams (Assistant Secretary of State for Latin America under Reagan) attacked the 'paralysis' induced by 'a system in which it is much easier to resist action than to act'. Abrams criticised rules introduced since Vietnam, such as the executive order prohibiting the assassination of heads of government, saying these made support for a coup virtually impossible.

However, there was no need to revise the post-Vietnam tests for the advisability of military intervention, since Panama by now had passed them all. The FDP was incapable of fighting a prolonged war against US forces; no foreign power would offer Noriega military assistance; the objectives of intervention were clear and — in theory at least — easily attainable; and, most important of all, the US public was in favour. Washington could therefore look forward to a swift and popular victory, followed by an orderly withdrawal with few US casualties. The only thing that remained was to apply the other major lesson learned in South East Asia; immediate, overwhelming force to achieve the total destruction of the enemy. The green light was given no later than early November, and under cover of regular supply flights, Southcom began shipping in tanks and assault helicopters. The countdown to Operation Just Cause had begun.

Chapter 2
Canals and Colonies

Despite the speeches and statements of US leaders, Manuel Noriega alone did not cause the crisis of 1987-89. Nor will his overthrow resolve Panama's underlying instability. The roots of the tragedy of December 1989 lie in the historical relationship between Panama and the US, and in the social and economic relations within the isthmus. Panama's uniquely distorted society was already established before its formal independence from Colombia in 1903.

From the beginning of the Spanish empire in the New World, Panama's importance lay in its geography. Until the 1730s, Panama had one of only three ports through which Spain authorised trade with the New World (the others being Lima and Vera Cruz). Through Panama, by human bearer and pack animal came the wealth extracted from the Pacific and inland provinces of South America. With this trade developed a prosperous community of merchants which, to the extent that the province of Panama had any autonomy, comprised the local ruling class. While elsewhere in Latin America the importance of the merchant class stemmed from the power of the large landowners, in Panama the merchant class ruled supreme.

The interior of the isthmus produced little during the first two centuries after the conquest. There were few settlements, no known mineral wealth of note, and no substantial indigenous population which could be recruited into forced labour for plantation agriculture or mining, as happened in Peru or Mexico. While forced labour estates (*encomiendas*) existed in Panama, the largest had no more than 30 or 40 workers and the colonial authorities abolished the system (formally at least) by the middle of the 17th century.

After the British destroyed the forts at Portobelo in 1739, accelerating the decline of the isthmus as a trading route, the dominant merchant class fell upon hard times. With the reduction in trade many poor families abandoned the towns to seek a livelihood in the hinterland, joining the descendants of black slaves who had been thrown onto the land when the short-lived gold-mining industry collapsed.

These settlers did not become a wealthy landed class. For the most part they remained subsistence producers. Alongside the poor peasants there emerged medium-sized, commercial farms, usually centred on cattle-raising. But these lacked importance both in terms of numbers and political influence.

While the class structure of Panama underwent important changes during the colonial period, and later under Colombian rule, these relationships remained at its heart up to Panama's secession from Colombia in 1903. An urban merchant class held political power, while the countryside was sparsely settled, largely by subsistence farmers.

In the 1840s the development of a regular steamship service revived the depressed fortunes of the Panama crossing, although further north competition came from Vanderbilt's route up the San Juan river and across Lake Nicaragua. Both routes boomed after gold was discovered in California in 1849. For gold prospectors from the US East Coast, the route across the isthmus was much less arduous than the trek across the US interior.

The cost advantage of the Panama route increased with the construction of a railway financed by New York entrepreneurs, begun in 1851 and completed in 1855. The railway brought great benefits to the Panamanian merchants, but it also established what became a permanent feature of their economic status: their relationship to trade across the isthmus was secondary to foreign (and increasingly, North American) domination over the means of transport.

By the eve of separation from Colombia the class structure of Panama had assumed the basic characteristics which would persist through the 20th century. On the isthmus political power was concentrated in the hands of an urban merchant class, which, although located at strategic points in the chain of commerce, did not control the key element in Panama's economic structure, namely the transport system. Thus, while the merchant class monopolised political power on the isthmus, it possessed virtually no direct economic control over the population.

Purely political control might have been effective had there been a political ideology capable of binding poor Panamanians to the urban elite. But until the emergence of the Arias brothers as a political force in the 1930s, no such ideology existed.

Ethnic divisions accentuated the fragile nature of the political control of the commercial class. Trans-shipment of commodities by human and animal power provided its profits. Many of the labourers were black: they had either come to the isthmus as slaves or fled there to escape slavery in the Caribbean. By the end of the 18th century Panama had a black majority, differentiated from the creole merchants both by class and culture.

More black labourers came to Panama to build the railway and for the French canal venture, mostly from the British Caribbean colonies. The white creole elite lived in fear of a black uprising like that which had expelled the French from Haiti, and in 1856 a riot by blacks in Panama City fuelled their anxieties.

Throughout the 19th century the creoles had vacillated over the issue of independence. On the one hand they resented the restrictions placed upon them by the central government in Bogotá, to which they had voluntarily subjected themselves after ties with Spain were cut. On the other, they feared that an independent Panama would be dominated by the poor majority over whom they exerted limited control.

During the Colombian civil war of 1840-41 the merchants declared independence from Colombia, but they lacked the military strength to defeat the central government. Again, during the presidency of Conservative Rafael Núñez in the 1880s, and the War of a Thousand Days (1899-1902) the notion of independence flourished, but was only resolved when outside forces — namely the US government — intervened.

Birth of a Nation

'I took the Isthmus, started the Canal and left Congress not to debate the Canal but to debate me.'
(President Theodore Roosevelt, 23 March 1911)

Much in the manner of Panama's acquisition of nationhood — while tinged with later tragedy — would not look out of place in a comic opera. For decades Washington had cast covetous glances at the Isthmus of Panama, seen as among the most suitable sites for an interoceanic canal. Such a canal would link the East and West coasts of the growing nation and bypass the difficult and costly overland route. The leader of the earliest survey expedition, Commander Thomas Selfridge of the US Navy, wrote: 'advantageous as an interoceanic canal would be to the commercial welfare of the whole world, it is doubly so for the necessities of American interests.'

Since independence from Spain in 1821, Panama had been a province of Colombia, even though overland communications between the two

— across the rainforests and swamps of the Darién gap — were virtually impossible.

In 1846 the US and Colombia signed the Bidlack Treaty, which granted the US rights of transit across Panama 'upon any modes of communication that now exist or that may be, hereafter, constructed'. The California gold rush began in 1849, well before the completion of a coast-to-coast US railway, making a trans-isthmian route a matter of urgency, and the privately-owned Panama Railroad Company took advantage of the circumstances.

When the railway opened for business in 1855 it proved a mixed blessing. While US citizens and the wealthier Panamanians benefited, railway construction workers lost their jobs once it had been built and other means of travel went bankrupt, bringing economic depression to the mass of the population.

Indirectly, these problems led to the first US military intervention in Panama, in 1856. The immediate flash-point was a slice of watermelon stolen by a US soldier. The resulting argument led to rioting in which over a dozen US citizens died. A few months later, 160 marines landed 'to protect the railroad'. The habit of intervention was to prove hard to break. The railway's heyday was a short one, however, for in 1869 the first railway line across the North American continent began operation.

In 1880, under the direction of Ferdinand de Lesseps, builder of the Suez Canal, the French *Compagnie Universelle du Canal Interocéanique* launched an attempt to build a sea level waterway through Panama. The French had obtained from Colombia the Wyse concession, a 99-year right to build and operate a canal, and they proceeded to buy out, at enormous cost, the Panama Railroad Company. The railway company remained US-based, and more importantly, the Bidlack Treaty guaranteeing US access to the isthmus remained in force.

Despite heroic efforts, costing thousands of labourers' lives, the French had to admit defeat after nine years which bankrupted the *Compagnie Universelle*. The effort foundered on a shortage of capital and the technological impossibility of building a sea-level, rather than a lock canal.

Washington, though preoccupied with the American civil war and its aftermath, had never accepted the notion of a canal controlled by Europeans. Further, the Spanish-American war of 1898 had convinced the US military of the need for a fast passage between the Atlantic and Pacific for its naval vessels. In 1903 the US and Colombia negotiated a fresh agreement, the Hay-Herrán Treaty. This granted the US the 'exclusive and absolute option' to build and operate a canal for a

The new Governor of Panama. "Say, boy, see if there's anybody out there that wants a treaty signed."   (*Daily Tribune*/Hulton-Deutsch)

100-year (potentially renewable) period; while Bogotá would retain sovereignty and the obligation to defend the canal militarily.

To the dismay of the North Americans, however, the Colombian senate refused to ratify the treaty. At this point Washington suddenly began to take an interest in the grumblings of the Panamanian secessionists, which it had hitherto ignored. However, it would be wrong to suggest that the secessionist movement was a mere invention of US politicians. The Panamanians chafed under the unenlightened rule of remote Bogotá, and there had been no less than 33 attempts to declare independence in the years since 1830. On two occasions — in 1841 and 1855 — the nationalists had briefly succeeded, only to be reabsorbed by their more powerful neighbour. The difference on this occasion was the US navy.

Philippe Bunau-Varilla deserves the title of midwife at the birth of Panama. A Frenchman who had served as director general of the canal excavation, Bunau-Varilla was a shareholder in the *Compagnie Nouvelle* which had emerged from the wreckage of the venture. He thus had a personal interest in a US buy-out of the French rights and assets.

Operating out of Room 1162 at the Waldorf Astoria in New York (which he later described, without a hint of irony, as 'the cradle of the Panama Republic'), Bunau-Varilla appointed himself intermediary between Washington and the secessionists. Greatly aided by the neo-imperialist aspirations of Roosevelt, who dropped heavy hints that the US would not stand idly by in the event of a secession, he convinced the leaders of the revolt to make their move.

'I do not think,' wrote Roosevelt at the time, 'that the Bogotá lot of jack rabbits should be allowed permanently to bar one of the future highways of civilization.' Weakened by the devastating War of a Thousand Days (1899-1902), the Colombians stood little chance, but having got wind of the rebel plans they succeeded in landing 500 troops at Colón. The contingent arrived shortly after the US gunboat *Nashville*, whose commander made no immediate attempt to interfere.

However, tricked into travelling to Panama City without his troops, Colombian commander General Juan Tobar and his aides were arrested by rebel soldiers. The Colombian troops were persuaded to leave without a fight, as the US landed 400 marines from another ship. At six o'clock on the evening of Panama's declaration of independence, secessionist leader Manuel Amador Guerrero sent a telegram to US Secretary of State John Hay, which read: 'Proclaimed independence of Isthmus without bloodshed. The Canal Treaty saved.'

The Burden of Empire

Without the military presence of the US — had there been no American gunboats standing offshore at Colón and Panama City — the Republic of Panama probably would not have lasted a week. Rear Admiral Henry Glass, for example, would conclude after a careful appraisal of the republic's capacity to defend itself that at the very most 600 men might have been furnished with adequate arms. Taft, on his first visit to Panama a year later, would describe its army as 'not much larger than the army on an opera stage.' Colombia, had it had free access from the sea, could have landed several thousand veteran troops on both sides of the Isthmus, just as the conspirators themselves had appreciated from the beginning. As it was, a Colombian force of some 2,000 men did attempt an overland march through the Darién wilderness, but ravaged by fever, they gave up and turned back.

The orders that sent Hubbard ashore at Colón, that secured the railroad, that started ten warships converging on Panama from points several thousands of miles off, had all emanated from the State, War, and Navy Building and were accredited to the Secretary of the Navy, William H Moody, or to Acting Secretary Charles Darling and to Secretary of State Hay or to Acting Secretary Loomis. But the responsibility for 'the dynamic solution of the Panama Question' (in the words of John Hay's biographer) rested entirely with Theodore Roosevelt, as Roosevelt himself would proudly acknowledge. 'I did not consult Hay or Root [Secretary of War Elihu Root], or anyone else as to what I did, because a council of war does not fight; and I intended to do the job once for all.'

The American flag would 'bring civilisation into the waste places of the earth,' he had declared in one of his speeches earlier in the year. The burden of empire was to advance liberty and order and material progress. 'We have no choice as to whether or not we shall play a great part in the world,' he had told another cheering crowd at San Francisco. 'That has been determined for us by fate . . .' They were popular words and very like those in *Nostromo*, a novel that was to appear less than a year after Panama became a republic. Joseph Conrad's tale of a Latin American revolution and of the self-deceptions men work with the words they summon to deceive others. 'We shall run the world's business whether the world likes it or not,' a San Francisco financier remarks early in the story. 'The world can't help it — and neither can we, I guess.'

David McCullough, *The Path Between the Seas*, Simon & Schuster, NY, 1977

The Price of Independence

Bunau-Varilla's role was far from over. He had guaranteed the rebel leaders (Manuel Amador, Tomás Arias, Federico Boyd and José Agustín Arango) at least $100,000 — out of his own pocket if necessary. This may have influenced their decision to name him 'envoy extraordinary and ambassador plenipotentiary' in Washington, a decision they would regret. This French citizen, who had not visited Panama for the previous 18 years, took it upon himself to draft and sign a US-Panamanian canal treaty before the special commission from Panama, charged with the same task, could reach the US capital.

The terms of the new treaty were breathtaking; so much so that even Secretary of State John Hay was moved to say that it was 'very satisfactory, vastly advantageous to the US and we must confess .. not so advantageous to Panama.'

This was an understatement. The key clause in the new treaty was Article III. This granted the US within an expanded canal zone (ten miles wide instead of six) 'all the rights, power and authority .. which [it] would possess and exercise if it were the sovereign of the territory ... to the entire exclusion of the exercise by the Republic of Panama of any such sovereign rights, power or authority.' It even granted Washington these rights 'in perpetuity'.

The SS *Ancon* becomes the first ship to pass through the Panama Canal, 15 August 1914.

In exchange for handing over its single most important asset, the new republic would receive $10 million, plus (after nine years) a $250,000 fee each year. The US agreed to guarantee Panamanian independence, but at the price of intervention — inside and outside the Canal Zone — whenever the US deemed it necessary to 'maintain order'.

Faced with the fury of the Panamanians at his outrageous behaviour, Bunau-Varilla warned that if the treaty were not ratified the US would withdraw its protection. This was a lie, but it had the desired effect. Less than a month after the declaration of independence, Panama's National Assembly ratified the treaty after an acrimonious debate.

Lest the Panamanians should get ideas above their station, the US authorities then proceeded, in 1904, to remove all Panamanian judges from the Canal Zone and force the new republic to abolish its army; a move enshrined in the Taft Agreement of that year. Bound hand and foot, Panama was now firmly under US domination.

The contradiction between a genuine secessionist movement and the achievement of independence as part of the construction of a US overseas empire was a tragedy from which Panamanian national self-respect has yet to recover. The treaty which no Panamanian signed created a US territory within the country from which Panamanians were excluded except as menial and low-skilled workers.

Split in two by a strip of alien territory, Panama was a client state of the US. Until 1936 it existed within a legal-diplomatic framework equivalent to protectorate status. Economically the country was overwhelmingly dependent on the US, and under the monetary convention of 1904 it adopted the US dollar (euphemistically dubbed the *balboa*) as its currency. In consequence, Panamanian governments could have no independent monetary policy; an extraordinary arrangement which loomed large during the Reagan administration's campaign to remove General Noriega.

Washington took full advantage of its right of intervention in the 33 years up to 1936, sending in troops on nine occasions to put down unrest, protect US business interests or ensure a favourable election result. Only with the General Treaty of Friendship and Co-operation of 1936 was the protectorate status abolished, and this treaty merely made the interventions less overt. In 1944 one US official candidly acknowledged that 'there has never been a successful change of government in Panama but that American authorities have been consulted beforehand.'

During this period, government remained almost exclusively in the hands of the ruling elite, sometimes referred to as the 'twenty families', whose political vehicle from 1912 was the Liberal Party. Changes of government resembled a political version of musical chairs.

Nationalism in every Latin American country is in part a reaction to the influence of the US. In Panama, anti-US feeling has been its very essence. For 80 years US control of the canal was a daily reminder of this influence, a permanent and visible affront to any patriot.

Unapproachable Estate

If you drive from Panama City to Colón, along the highway magnificently called the Carretera Transístmica, you are travelling more or less parallel with the canal, without entering the Canal Zone (for a Treaty modification of 1955 kindly allowed the Panamanians to have a road of their own across the isthmus). Everything is highly Panamanian. The villages you pass through are cheerfully wayward, littered with 7-Up signs, buses with pictures, banana-sellers' booths and ravaged, abandoned automobiles. The country is jungly, hummocky and unlovely. There is a kind of aimless shabbiness to it all, shambled, benevolent but not picturesque. At one or two places, though, a side road will take you to a vantage point above the canal itself, and there,

(Courtesy of *Dialogo Social*, March 1974)

spread out before you between the hills, you may see an almost allegorical antithesis. There the tiled houses of the Americans nestle in their gardens. There the big ships sail across Gatún Lake, their high funnels and superstructures gliding grandly among the islands. There are the trim installations of USGOG or AMPLIG or COMSWAM. There everything seems cool, ordered, prosperous and private. It is like looking through the lodge gates at some unapproachable estate.

'An Imperial Specimen', Jan Morris, 1975, from the anthology *Destinations*, OUP, 1982

Arnulfo Arias and the Canal

While the canal was a symbol of frustrated sovereignty for Panamanians, for the US government it embodied overwhelming national security interests. From 1903 until the 1960s the basic US policy goal in Panama was that no government hold power that would challenge US control of the canal.

For this reason Arnulfo Arias Madrid (1901-88), the most popular politician in the history of Panama, was anathema to Washington. Because of his frequently anti-American rhetoric, Arias suffered hostile treatment in the US press. At one time he manifested fascist sentiments and held bizarre views on many subjects, including race. The same can be said, however, of other Latin American politicians whom US policymakers have embraced as allies. Washington's fundamental objection to Arias was not his fascism nor his racism, but that he demanded a revision of the canal treaties.

For over 50 years Arias encapsulated nationalist frustration over the canal issue, despite his distinctly patchy record on the question. As Raúl Leis pointed out in the Panamanian magazine *Diálogo Social* in 1983, while in exile in the US in the 1970s Arias 'opposed negotiations [for the Torrijos-Carter treaties], and lent support and collaboration to the campaign by the most reactionary groups in that country who argued that the canal was being handed over to communists.' At this time he became firm friends with the governor of California, Ronald Reagan.

Arias was first elected president in 1940 and several times subsequently, the most recent occasion being in 1984 when he was defrauded of victory and Nicolás Ardito Barletta declared the winner. At the time of his death he was the favourite to win the election of 1989 (when he would have been 87). But of the 14 years he should theoretically have served as president, he only managed 31 months: each time he won, some permutation of his three main enemies — the oligarchy, the National Guard and the US embassy — contrived to remove him from office.

Arias' decades-long hold over the Panamanian electorate rested on two factors. He built his career on the canal issue, and his power base lay among the poor, who had largely remained outside the rather weak and ineffectual labour movement. This political alliance with the nationalist masses threatened the narrow structure of Panamanian politics.

Arias' political movement (formally structured into the *Panameñista* Party in 1960) gave expression to the class and ethnic divisions in Panama, while the politicians of the conservative, upper-class parties were never able to win mass support and relied on fraud and coups to keep him from power. It is one of the many quirks of Panamanian history that the coup of 1968 which broke the upper-class monopoly on political power was carried out against Arnulfo Arias. In contrast to his nationalist platform and working-class power base, the upper classes and their political parties came to be seen as collaborators with the US.

Further, the Panamanian elite is for the most part white and of European descent (Endara, Arias Calderón and Ford, the current ruling troika, being prime examples), while the ethnic composition of poor Panamanians is much more heterogeneous. When, in 1987, the elite launched its all-out effort to dislodge Noriega from power, its long history of exploitative relations and contempt for working people greatly hindered its appeal. Throughout most of the history of Panama as a nominally independent nation, the government of the US sided with the elite. Until 1968 this alliance reflected a narrow interpretation of the nature of Panamanian politics: to maintain US control over the canal it was necessary to prevent Arias from becoming president. In 1941, the US government actively co-operated in overthrowing Arias after his first election victory, and it encouraged his fall in 1948.

Arias' own origins were European and he came from farming stock. His ideology was a ragbag of nationalism (what he termed *panameñismo*), xenophobia, anti-communism and social reformism (he introduced female suffrage, for example). He drew his support from all those groups in Panamanian society who felt excluded by the commercial elite. In the last two decades of his life, however, he focused his hostility primarily on the National Guard/FDP, and his policies when in government never confronted the interests of the elite, with whom the remnants of his movement are now firmly aligned.

His governments included members of some of the wealthiest families, and both his rhetoric and his actions were profoundly anti-communist. In 1950, for instance, he banned left-wing parties, and in 1964 he condemned the flag riots as the work of 'local agents of international communism'. Moreover, despite his populist political platforms, he used his presidencies to accumulate substantial personal wealth.

During the 1950s Arias was out of active politics. When he ran again and lost through fraud in 1964, Washington made no protest and quickly recognised the new president. In 1968 the Johnson administration applauded the military coup that overthrew him after barely a week in office.

In 1984 the US moved swiftly to endorse Arias' opponent, Nicolás Ardito Barletta, who was declared the winner of the fraudulent election. The perpetrator of the electoral fraud was none other than Manuel Noriega, whom the US had aided to become commander of the FDP the year before.

The Torrijos Years

'We are too apt to class together the generals of South and Central America. Torrijos was a lone wolf.'
(Graham Greene, *Getting to Know the General*)

When Arnulfo Arias became president of Panama for the third time, in 1968, the leaders of the National Guard were not pleased. They had done their best to rig the election against him, but he had won a 'Panamanian victory' — defined as one big enough to outweigh the effects of ballot-rigging. A split in the elite between the technocratic, reformist elements, who supported President Kennedy's Alliance for Progress, and those who opposed reform at all costs, had allowed the veteran populist another chance in government. It lasted 11 days.

Arias fell because he attempted to curb the power of the National Guard (*Guardia Nacional*, or GN). Just a few days after his inauguration he announced that the Presidential Guard was no longer under the GN high command but would henceforth be directly answerable to his own aide-de-camp, Lieutenant Colonel Romero Duque. To make matters worse, he attempted a major reshuffle of the GN leadership, moving its two most important officers — Lieutenant Colonel Omar Torrijos and Major Boris Martínez — to minor posts. Arias tried to banish Torrijos to El Salvador as military attaché, and ordered Martínez to the rural backwater of Chitré. In the event, it was Arias who had to pack his bags, and flee in humiliating fashion to Miami via the Canal Zone.

It was not immediately clear what the military coup would mean for Panama. The elite assumed that power would swiftly be returned to them, but the GN was no longer their passive tool. This time it was acting on its own behalf. General Bolívar Vallarino, the retiring GN commander, proved to be the last member of the oligarchy to hold that post, and Lieutenant Colonel Federico Boyd — also a scion of the '20 families' and now their most senior GN representative — was soon on a plane out of the country himself.

The GN outlawed political parties and dissolved the National Assembly. An initial promise of elections within three months was quietly dropped and the prisons began to fill up with opponents of all ideological complexions. But Torrijos and Martínez proved unable to work together, despite the coincidence of some of their aims. Torrijos, whose parents were teachers and who had trained at the Salvadorean military academy, was a negotiator, while the Mexican-trained Martínez preferred confrontation.

The crunch came after only a few months, when Martínez, without consulting Torrijos, announced on television that the military regime would be embarking on a radical programme including agrarian reform. The next day Martínez was off to a new life in Miami, where he eventually found work in the freight department of TACA, the Salvadorean airline. Washington, happy to see the back of a dangerous radical, gave Torrijos a hand with his removal. Indeed, according to US journalist Seymour Hersh, writing in *Life* magazine in March 1990, the 470th US Military Intelligence Group played a part in the overthrow of Arias, thereby earning a place as the new government's favourite among the nine different US intelligence organisations operating in Panama at the time.

It was not long, however, before the Nixon administration began to realise that it might have swapped one 'communist' for another in easing the departure of Martínez. The CIA in particular was unhappy, since the 470th had cornered the market in intelligence contacts, and to restore what it felt was its rightful status it paid chief of staff Colonel Amado Sanjur $100,000 to overthrow Torrijos.

The plotters came close to succeeding. Torrijos was in Mexico at the time, and it was only the loyalty of some of his subordinates (notably Lieutenant Colonel Manuel Antonio Noriega) which allowed him to stage a successful return. In the event, he landed at David near the Costa Rican border (in the military zone controlled by Noriega) and drove in triumph, amid cheering crowds, to the capital. The date on which the counter-coup was crushed became known as 'Loyalty Day', and Noriega, his career built on his correct choice of sides, declared it a public holiday when he came to power in 1983.

Seymour Hersh wrote that the coup attempt 'was triggered not by Panamanians but by bitter bureaucratic infighting between the 470th and the CIA. The struggle was not over a question of US policy — what would be best for the government and people of Panama — but over turf; whether the Army or the CIA would become the pre-eminent intelligence agency in Panama.' Whatever the reasons, the threat was over, and the way now clear for Torrijos.

Panama's new ruler defined the guiding principles of his regime in an interview with the novelist Gabriel García Márquez, published in 1975. He dismissed 'ideological refinements which are always open to the charge of lacking an indigenous character ... We don't follow a set of ideological rules, for we would run the risk of being narrowly patriotic without being truly nationalistic.' His government, the general said, placed more emphasis on concrete goals and achievements than on political labels. The most important of these was the recovery of control over the canal for Panama. This was, *par excellence*, an issue capable of uniting Panamanians of all classes and political persuasions — although from his US exile Arnulfo Arias lined up with the US far right who argued that the waterway should not be handed over to 'a bunch of communists'.

Asked by García Márquez to demonstrate the 'revolutionary nature' of his regime, Torrijos pointed to the nationalisation of electricity and communications; the establishment of state corporations in the banana, sugar and cement sectors; and the creation of agricultural and urban transport co-operatives. In the field of social legislation he picked out the new labour code, educational and housing reforms, and the promotion of trade union organisations.

In its early years, the Torrijos regime substantially improved the lives of ordinary Panamanians, achieving a degree of social integration undreamed-of during the years of rule by the *rabiblancos* ('white-arses') of the traditional elite. The 1972 labour code embodied the radical, reforming character of the early years; years in which union leaders enjoyed a privileged relationship with the regime, including posts in the government. For the first time, collective bargaining and the right to strike were enshrined in law; job security was guaranteed after two years' employment and a national workers' consultative council (CONATO) was established.

However, the labour code was the high-water mark of the Torrijos reforms, and soon private enterprise, led by the employers' organisation (CONEP), turned the tide. The revision of the labour code under Law 95 of 1976 was a response both to economic decline (due in part to global factors such as the oil crisis which were outside the regime's control) and to Torrijos' belief that he needed to keep the business class on his side if he was to win the battle for the canal.

With some justification, he evidently felt that the trade unions would back him anyway, because of the lack of alternatives. Angel Gómez, secretary-general of the National Confederation of Workers (CNT), admitted in later years that, 'we were careful not to sharpen the struggle at home because the principal objective in our programme was passage of the treaties'.

Nevertheless, many trade unionists naturally developed a sense of betrayal at the regime's failure to acknowledge this support. In 1978, the secretary-general of the Confederation of Workers of the Republic of Panama (CTRP), Phillip Butcher, noted that, 'in 1972 there was more unity between the government and workers because the government had not yet established good relations with the capitalist class. So it needed support from the working class to stay in power. The bosses are now on good terms with the government and have imposed their terms on the workers'.

The thread running through the Torrijos years was the attempt to achieve capitalist modernisation by means of a national project involving both workers and peasants, and elements of the private sector. Torrijos was not a socialist, much less a communist, although he did succeed in winning over to his cause the Moscow-line People's Party after initial hostility on both sides. The PPP held government posts and remained loyal to *torrijismo* even after the general's death.

The military regime transformed the economy of Panama in ways which delighted the merchants who had always been the most important element among the domestic business community. Strict banking secrecy was introduced, allowing the creation of a booming International Financial Centre, which at its peak accommodated over 130 banks. Torrijos set up the Colón free trade zone, which swiftly rose to occupy second place in the world, outranked only by Hong Kong. Both these developments accentuated the existing peculiarities of the Panamanian economy, with its dependence (via the canal) on servicing other people's productive activities, rather than promoting its own. Since colonial times the isthmus had served primarily as a transit zone: Torrijos took that trend to extremes.

Torrijos did attempt to revive domestic production, but his efforts largely failed. An agrarian reform programme (1969-77), for example, benefited only one in ten rural families and failed to halt the increase in landlessness. By the time Torrijos met his death, in 1981, production was declining not only in agriculture but in manufacturing and construction as well.

The Torrijos government expanded public services, such as housing, transportation and health, at the cost of increasing indebtedness, and when interest rate rises began to bite in the early 1980s the economy ground to a halt. By 1983 Panama had one of the highest per capita debt levels in the world and its $3.4 billion foreign debt represented over three quarters of its gross domestic product (GDP).

Battle for the Canal

'I don't want to enter the history books. I want to enter the Canal Zone.'
(General Omar Torrijos)

'We bought it, we paid for it, it's ours, and we should tell Torrijos and company that we are going to keep it.'
(Ronald Reagan)

The fight to change the grossly unjust terms of the 1903 Canal Treaty dominated the Torrijos years. A glance at the nature of this foreign enclave in the middle of Panama — 'a stake in our heart' as Torrijos himself called it — makes it easy to understand why its existence grated on Panamanian nationalist sensibilities.

After the ratification of the 1903 Canal Treaty, the US proceeded to obliterate from the Canal Zone all vestiges of Panamanian control. The Zone was a 640 square mile strip running right through Panama, dividing the country in two. Its governor was invariably a general from the US Corps of Engineers, who also headed the Canal Company. It had its own police force and courts and a system of racial segregation which outlasted the abolition of racist laws in the southern US. As Graham Greene noted, 'if you were a Panamanian you had to exercise caution, for if you were involved in a traffic offence on the wrong side of the street you would be judged in an American court by American law.'

In this tropical enclave, with its neatly mowed lawns, swimming pools and white picket fences, native Panamanians were tolerated rather than welcomed. US citizens earned three or four times as much as Panamanians doing the same jobs. From 1903 to 1959 it was actually illegal to fly the Panamanian flag inside the Zone. In 1963 President Kennedy decreed that a Panamanian flag could fly wherever the Stars and Stripes was displayed.

The Colour of Your Money

You arrived at the Balboa airport in the Canal Zone hot and thirsty and cast around for a water fountain. When you had drunk the edge off your thirst, you raised your eyes and saw stencilled on the wall: Gold only.

'My, what a strange error,' you mused. 'Surely they mean "cold only".' Then it occurred to you that no water fountain is equipped with hot water. Your mind chewed on the riddle.

As you came across the women's and men's rooms on the way out, you encountered the same ominous Gold only. Midas, surely, had been left far behind. Later, you discovered two sets of wickets in Canal Zone Post Offices, Gold and Silver. You awakened to the fact that it was Jim Crow in the tropics, glazed over with a thin hypocrisy that if anything made it more revolting. Below the Mason-Dixon Line it had the merit of being forthright.

Alongside the canal, a monument to his capacity for wrestling with material obstacles, man had created a snarl of social problems. We join oceans and set up barriers between man and man.

The North Americans, like the French before them, found that British West Indian Negroes were indispensable for the building of the canal. They had tried Chinese, Irish, and Panamanian Negroes, but these either fell victim to disease or were lazy or undisciplined. From Jamaica came tractable blacks, hardworking and relatively immune to the deadly germs that infested the canal route. Under the French no racial problem had arisen from the immigration of tens of thousands of Jamaicans: they tended to assimilate with the Panamanians who, having much Negro blood themselves, were not bitten by racial prejudice.

But then the French went bankrupt and the US took over. For some obscure reason most of the straw bosses sent down were Southerners, perhaps because they were more inured to the climate; possibly, as in the case of Haiti, because they were felt to have experience in 'handling' Negroes. Or it may simply have been the working of that unwritten social law that prompts every nation to step outside its own frontiers with its worse foot. In any case the Southern straw bosses brought with them their peculiar convictions as to how society ought to be run.

It was quite out of the question to introduce an open system of Jim Crow in Panama, where so much black blood is mingled with even the bluest streams. So they took a page from William Jennings Bryan, and resorted to bimetallism. The labourers, accustomed to silver currencies, were paid in silver; the US technicians and straw bosses received greenbacks, that is, gold. The knavery of the human heart appealed to the resourceful cowardice of the mind, and the unspeakable thing was covered up with a new set of words — the 'gold and silver rolls'. Gold and silver commissaries, toilets, dispensaries, schools, Post Office wickets, and other novel things — some even unknown in the US South — came into existence.

William Krehm, *Democracies and Tyrannies in the Caribbean*, 1948.

The Zonians, effectively settlers born and brought up in the canal strip, were in no hurry to put the new rule into practice. Many of them were rabidly anti-Panamanian, and on 9 January 1964 the simmering resentment of Panamanians at their second-class status in a part of their own country boiled over. The Zone authorities had delayed their compliance with the 'two flags' principle, and in order to reduce the number of Panamanian flags which had to be raised they ordered the dismantling of a number of flagpoles. This in turn met with resistance from Zonians, who in some cases placed round-the-clock guards on their flags.

When a group of Panamanian students peacefully attempted to raise the national flag at the Balboa High School, Zonians attacked them and tore the flag down. What followed became known as the 'flag riots';

three days of demonstrations that left 21 Panamanians and four US soldiers dead. Most of the victims died in the El Chorrillo district (which was to suffer the greatest losses in the 1989 invasion), and the main street running past El Chorrillo was later renamed Avenue of the Martyrs.

The Liberal government of Roberto Chiari felt compelled to break off diplomatic relations with Washington (which had blamed the trouble on 'professional agitators'), and ties were only restored after mediation by the Organization of American States. The Panamanian ambassador to the UN said, 'The present status of the Canal Zone, which is and will be a source of daily and permanent discord, must be altered. Panama cannot remain subject to unfair treaties imposed against its legitimate rights and injurious to its very existence as a nation.'

At the end of 1964 US President Lyndon Johnson announced that negotiations for a new canal treaty would take place. Modifications to the 1903 treaty had already been introduced. In 1936 Washington had given up its right of unilateral intervention in Panama except where necessary to defend the canal. In 1955 the US had increased its annuity and introduced theoretical wage equality. The one-sided nature of the relationship was underlined, however, by further Panamanian concessions on both occasions.

In 1936 Panama handed over additional areas of its territory that Washington deemed necessary for the defence and modernisation of the canal; in 1955 it gave 8,000 hectares, rent-free for 15 years, for use as a US military base. The 1942 US-Panama Base Convention further allowed the US to install over 100 military and telecommunications facilities in furtherance of the US war effort.

The new talks proceeded slowly, and the two sides finally drafted a set of three new treaties in 1967. The Johnson administration had shown little enthusiasm for the process, and hinted that the Panama Canal might soon be obsolete anyway, since the US was planning a sea-level canal, probably through Nicaragua. The 1967 draft would have perpetuated US control until 2067, affirmed the legality of the US military bases (whose presence could only be justified under the 1903 treaty as 'fortifications' to protect the canal), and given the US the exclusive right to build a sea-level canal in Panama. Johnson's decision not to seek a second term, together with Panamanian hostility to the terms of the treaties, helped ensure they were never ratified.

The 1968 coup which brought Torrijos to power was the final nail in the coffin of these proposals. The new Panamanian leader refused to accept the draft treaties even as a basis for discussion (his foreign minister described them as 'even more offensive than the Treaty of

General Omar Torrijos   (Carlos Reyes, ANDES Press Agency)

1903 itself'). Instead, Torrijos raised the international profile of the canal issue to apply pressure on Washington. Seeking support from among his Latin American neighbours, the non-aligned nations, and even major allies of the US, Torrijos persuaded the UN Security Council to convene a special session in Panama City in March 1973, despite US protests.

The Security Council session passed a resolution favourable to Panama, which was duly vetoed by the US, thereby confirming its international isolation on the issue. The UK, which abstained, was the only other country not to vote in favour. Less than a year later, US Secretary of State Henry Kissinger and Panamanian Foreign Minister Juan Antonio Tack put their signatures to an eight point Agreement on Principles which established the framework for the treaty negotiations. This included the statement that the 'concept of perpetuity will be eliminated'.

At this point, in the run-up to the 1976 US elections, the canal issue became a rallying cry for the US right, and in particular for the governor of California, Ronald Reagan, a contender for the Republican presidential nomination. The furore delayed further progress until after Jimmy Carter's inauguration in January 1977. Ironically, the right helped Carter to victory by refusing to vote for his Republican opponent Gerald Ford, who backed the treaty negotiations.

Carter realised that the US needed to reach a speedy conclusion on the Panama issue. The canal was almost indefensible against possible sabotage, the threat of which was bound to increase without an agreement. Washington's main concern was to ensure the continued presence of US military bases, which played a vital role in maintaining US control in the hemisphere. Not only were they the springboard for virtually every US military intervention in Latin America this century but their sophisticated monitoring equipment enabled surveillance to be carried out against targets as far away as Chile.

Two treaties were signed within eight months of Carter's inauguration, on 7 September 1977, and ratified by a whisker (68-32 on an issue requiring a two-thirds majority) by the US Senate the following year. In addition to the provisions regarding canal revenues, the US also agreed, outside of the treaty framework, to contribute loans and credits, (mainly to new US investors), as well as a ten-year military assistance programme.

Moreover, the treaties did at least provide for the canal to be handed over to Panama on 31 December 1999 and for most of the Zone to revert almost immediately to Panamanian control; a transfer of 64 per cent of its land area (including the railway and the ports at either end) which took place on 1 October 1979. Although the US retained unilateral rights of intervention, Torrijos insisted on a Statement of Understanding, which prevented Washington from interfering in Panama's internal affairs. Panama, it seemed, was finally a sovereign state.

The Carter-Torrijos Treaties 1977

The following are the main provisions of the Panama Canal Treaty and the Treaty on the Permanent Neutrality and Operation of the Panama Canal:

● the Canal Zone ceased to exist and Panama assumed territorial jurisdiction
● the US retained the right to operate the canal until the year 2000, but under a newly-created, nine-member Panama Canal Commission (five US and four Panamanian citizens)
● Panama would gradually assume greater control over the canal, and in 1990 a Panamanian would become Canal Administrator (head of the Commission)
● an increasing percentage of canal tolls would go to Panama

● no sea-level canal would be built in Panama without US consent; there would be no US negotiations on a sea-level canal with any other Western Hemisphere nation

● key US military bases and training areas would remain under US control until the year 2000

● the canal would be 'permanently neutral'; the primary responsibility for canal defence would rest with US military until that year; the US would retain authority to intervene thereafter in defence of canal neutrality.

● a memorandum of understanding attached to the treaties made it clear that the US had no right of intervention in Panama's internal affairs.

The implementation of the treaties ran far from smoothly, even before the onset of the crisis in US-Panamanian relations in 1987. The Panamanian authorities criticised the implementing legislation passed by the US Congress (Public Law 96-70) as violating the spirit and letter of the Carter-Torrijos accords. Panama's principal objections to PL 96-70 centred on the distribution of canal profits and on labour policy. Torrijos argued that the treaties required profits up to $10 million to be handed over, while the canal administration said US law required it not to make a profit. By October 1986 the Panamanians reckoned the US owed them $64 million.

The Panamanian authorities also complained that US workers were still getting the best jobs and earning better salaries and fringe benefits than those of Panamanians. Joint commissions and informal agreements resolved many of these complaints, but there remained a lingering resentment and a widespread belief that Washington was looking for ways to keep its soldiers in Panama after the year 2000.

Changing the Guard

In the years following the 1968 coup the National Guard became Panama's most important political institution. This remained so up to the 1989 invasion, even after the nominal reinstatement of civilian government in 1980. The US, which in 1989 would go to war against the GN's successor, the FDP, played a major part in its development.

A battalion of Colombian troops formed the nucleus of the post-independence Panamanian armed forces, together with the Colombian gunships which had been in the harbour at Panama City on the day the new republic declared its independence. The nationalists had bribed their officers and men to change sides.

Training session in the Canal Zone's School of the Americas, where many of Latin America's future military dictators went to study   (ANDES Press Agency)

However, as early as November 1904 Washington succeeded in forcing the newborn republic to abolish its army, replacing it with a virtually powerless police force which was itself disarmed ten years later. For the first three decades of its existence Panama was in all but name a US protectorate, with Washington controlling not only national defence but also internal policing and security. With the 'demilitarisation' of Panama in 1990 history repeated itself, for in the 1910s, the US government disarmed the Panamanian National Police, allowing it only handguns and parade rifles without firing pins. This arrangement formally came to an end in 1936. During World War II, again as a result of US pressure, the government first militarised the National Police, then in 1953 upgraded it into a National Guard.

The US helped shape the National Guard through military assistance and training. In the absence of a Panamanian military academy, the School of the Americas in the Canal Zone trained over 5,000 National Guard members before it moved to Fort Benning, Georgia, in 1984. This figure represents one in nine of all trainees, making Panama the third largest user of the School, despite the small size of its armed forces. It was not the only influence, however. Officers also received training in Chile, Colombia, Mexico, El Salvador, Peru and Venezuela;

and although Pentagon thinking held sway in some of these countries, each also had its own military tradition.

Prior to 1968 there was a close identification of interests between the governing elite and the National Guard, whose commanding officers themselves came mostly from the ruling class. A policy of discrimination ensured that ordinary Panamanians, and particularly non-white soldiers, failed to reach the upper ranks.

General Torrijos' assumption of power after the 1968 coup broke the elite's control over the GN. Most of the Guard (which numbered around 6,000 at that time) consisted of blacks and mestizos who were sympathetic to Torrijos' social aims. Torrijos himself came from a middle class mestizo family, the son of teachers. Many of his successors in the 1980s in the upper ranks of the FDP were also of humble origins, including Manuel Antonio Noriega, an illegitimate mestizo child of the slums.

The 1972 constitution, introduced by Torrijos, made the National Guard the country's principal political institution. Torrijos received the title of 'maximum leader of the Panamanian revolution'. In the first ten years of his government he boosted GN forces to 15,000 and increased its budget tenfold. As it grew in size and power, the Guard came increasingly to represent its own interests, forging tactical alliances with other social groups for particular purposes. The Guard's independence grew with the creation in 1983 (after Noriega's assumption of command) of the Panama Defence Forces (FDP), incorporating not only the National Guard but also the tiny navy and air force, the police, the Canal Defence Force, the traffic department and the immigration service.

Washington saw the upgrading and restructuring of the National Guard as an essential element in the process of handing over the canal to Panama; always assuming that the new-style armed forces could remain firmly under US influence and control. The detailed plans owed a great deal to Noriega's adviser Mike Harari, a former member of the Israeli intelligence agency Mossad; the name 'Defence Forces' was copied from the Israeli armed forces. Noriega increased the size of the military and improved its equipment and facilities, leaving the FDP more dependent than ever on US military aid. Law 20, which the Assembly rubber-stamped soon after Noriega took over the Guard/ FDP, formalised this new structure. It also placed control of airports and port facilities — including customs and immigration — in the hands of the FDP and ensured that the civilian authorities would be unable to invoke any statute in seeking to bring the military under control. No FDP commander would be subject to dismissal by the president of the republic. Strangely, President Delvalle seems to have ignored this point when he attempted to dismiss Noriega in 1988.

Noriega appointed military officers, both active service and retired, to head a number of governmental or semi-governmental bodies. Apart from the aviation and port authorities, these included agencies as diverse as the Institute of Renewable Natural Resources and the education ministry's Office of Student Affairs. Significantly, they also included DEPAT (Executive Directorate for Treaty Affairs), the support agency for Panama's representatives on the bilateral canal body. This caused Christian Democrat leader Ricardo Arias Calderón to conclude that Noriega had a 'new concept of the role of the military regarding the canal', and that he might even be preparing for 'military operation of the canal'.

Of the many ironies in the relationship between the US and Panama, perhaps the most striking is the central role played by Washington in creating and nurturing the National Guard/FDP, the dragon it felt obliged to slay in 1989. Throughout the previous four decades, Washington had seen the Panamanian military — in which it had striven to implant its own attitudes —as the best guarantee of stability for the country and, more importantly, the canal.

Washington therefore raised no objections when the Guard responded to Arnulfo Arias' attempt in 1968 to curb its power by overthrowing him. It backed Omar Torrijos and kept quiet when Torrijos' successors employed fraud to ensure victory for their candidate in 1984. Its support for the FDP, via military assistance, joint exercises and so on, effectively undermined the authority of the civilian government. The latter had to compete — for example — with the FDP's 'civic action programmes', such as health and community development projects, which were funded by the US and whose primary function was to strengthen the military's role in society.

From mid-1987, even after the relationship with Noriega had broken down, the US clung to the idea that removing the commander-in-chief would suffice to restore the FDP's respectability. Washington turned a deaf ear to the protests of the opposition, who wanted a much more comprehensive reappraisal of military involvement in politics.

As Arias Calderón (later to become first vice-president of Panama) put it in a 1987 article for the US quarterly Foreign Affairs: 'The US has considered the Panamanian Defence Forces as the most important factor for Panama's stability, and thus the domestic agent which could most affect the canal's security. It has sought, therefore, to have a close, positive relationship with the military leadership, regardless of other considerations. Human rights and democratisation have been at best a secondary priority ...'

As was the question of eradicating corruption in the military, a phenomenon which Torrijos had done little to discourage, apparently seeing it as a way to avoid discontent among his subordinates. By 1985 the FDP was aptly described (in a US senate staffers' report) as 'the axel around which the wheel of corruption turns.'

In a now notorious phrase, contained in a March 1988 statement rightly interpreted as an appeal to Panamanian officers to overthrow Noriega, US Secretary of State George Shultz referred to the FDP as 'a strong and honourable force that has a significant and proper role to play' in a future Panama. The FDP's proven record of corruption, repression and drug trafficking was no obstacle as long as Washington needed it.

In his book *Divorcing the Dictator*, Fred Kempe of the *Wall Street Journal* notes, 'in the 1960s officers had been relatively poor and humble. By the late 1970s, even lower-level officers were driving expensive cars, keeping two or three mistresses, and finding that their sources of income were limited only by their postings and imaginations.'

Several factors made it relatively simple to skim off enormous quantities of money. They included the growth of Panama's role as a haven for funds of dubious, and even straightforwardly criminal, origin; its geographical position as a hub of world commerce and a neighbour of Colombia, the world's premier cocaine producer; and the guerrilla wars further up the isthmus of Central America, which created a lucrative arms market.

By the time Washington decided to overthrow Noriega, and settled on the FDP as its chosen agent, it was hard for the US to compete with the patronage and bribery which the commander-in-chief could offer. Every FDP officer above the rank of major could make twice and three times his salary by taking advantage of his position.

When Colonel Roberto Díaz Herrera, Noriega's former second-in-command, was ousted in mid-1987, he not only accused Noriega of corruption on a grand scale but also confessed to it himself; and we may assume that in this he was not exaggerating. He bought his house, in the exclusive Altos del Golf district, with the proceeds of visa sales to Cubans trying to enter the US.

The other major complication, by the time the removal of Noriega had become Washington's top priority, was the parallel command structure he had introduced. Aided by his 11 years as head of military intelligence (G2), and by his Israeli advisers (who handled his personal security), Noriega used his closest allies to spy on less trusted officers. This network, its loyalty ensured by its members' complicity in large-scale corruption, enabled him to bypass the institutional command structure whenever necessary.

The extent to which the upper echelons of the FDP had become compromised by corruption was shown when the post-invasion regime purged every colonel and lieutenant-colonel, along with most of the majors, in order to reshape the FDP into the new Public Force.

For 20 years the military ruled Panama, a military fostered and nurtured by the US. Had he been so disposed, Manuel Noriega could have said with some truth, 'Washington made me what I am'. Only when the Reagan-Bush administration set about destroying its creation did it discover how well entrenched Noriega had become. Perhaps, deep in the bowels of the CIA building or the Pentagon, some of Noriega's former mentors took secret pride in their erstwhile client's extraordinary tenacity.

Chapter 3
Our Man in Panama

The military's dominance of Panamanian politics was inextricably linked with the careers of two individuals: Omar Torrijos Herrera and Manuel Antonio Noriega Morena.

For a man whose name became a household word, Noriega's early life was inauspicious, and he tried hard to keep its details secret while he was in power. Born in 1934, the offspring of a brief liaison between a lower-middle-class accountant and his domestic servant, he was brought up by his godmother in the slums of Panama City. Although he was physically small and suffered in his teenage years from the acne that left him permanently scarred, he compensated by developing his mental agility.

At school he was both well-behaved and above average academically, and at the age of 12 he won a place at the *Instituto Nacional* high school. Here he discovered that his father had other sons, and that one of them — Luis Carlos — attended the same school.

This stroke of luck helped determine the course of his life. Manuel Antonio and Luis Carlos got on well, and under his half-brother's influence the future dictator became prominent in the National Students' Congress and the socialist youth movement. According to Roberto Eisenmann, editor of the strongly anti-Noriega paper *La Prensa*, his lengthy relationship with US intelligence 'began probably in his mid-high school years . . . he started reporting to the CIA on the leftist students in the high school.' Former US Army intelligence officer Efraín Angueira (quoted by Seymour Hersh, *op cit*), agreed: 'We recruited him in high school for $25 a month,' adding, 'I remember taking him to the airport and giving him $20 when he left Panama for military school in Peru.'

Having failed to get into medical school, and after five years of dead-end jobs, the young Noriega took advantage of his half-brother's position in the Panamanian embassy in Lima. Luis Carlos was able to pull strings and falsify documents to gain Manuel Antonio's admission to the Chorrillos Military Academy. Here he provided intelligence reports on fellow cadets, having been recruited for the US embassy by Luis Carlos, whose socialist principles were evidently also skin-deep.

In Lima, Noriega's brutal streak became apparent both to his contemporaries at the academy and to his US contacts. Readers of Mario Vargas Llosa's novel *La Ciudad y los Perros* will recall that brutality was not in any way alien to Peruvian military academies. Lacking the money to pay for the services of a local prostitute, Noriega beat her severely until she gave in to him. Although he was arrested for the offence, it does not seem to have affected either his military career or his relations with US intelligence. Similar incidents recur in tales of his later years as a National Guard officer.

On returning to Panama in 1962, Noriega rapidly gained a commission as a second lieutenant. Chance sent him to the garrison at Colón, the city at the Atlantic end of the canal, where he came under the command of future coup leader Major Omar Torrijos. Their careers were henceforth indissolubly linked, until Torrijos's death in a plane crash almost 20 years later.

Torrijos found Noriega irreplaceable as a subordinate. Despite his often unsavoury behaviour, both on- and off-duty, he fulfilled any order, however difficult, and stayed loyal to those he felt could assist his advancement. When the High Command transferred Torrijos to run the Northern Zone, on the Panama-Costa Rica border, he took Noriega with him, and the young officer soon had the chance to practise political repression on supporters of Arnulfo Arias, whose home base lay in the area.

So enthusiastically did he carry out his task that Torrijos had to relieve him of his duties for ten days after complaints of brutality. Nonetheless, in recognition of his talents, Torrijos gave Noriega the task of setting up in the Northern Zone the National Guard's first genuine intelligence operation. This proved to be his true vocation, and of all the many courses he took in US military establishments, Noriega excelled at intelligence and counter-intelligence.

When Torrijos and Martínez seized power in 1968, Noriega backed them, and he rapidly gained promotion to commander of the Northern Zone. In this position he took perhaps his single most important step up the career ladder, by facilitating Torrijos' return to the country during the coup attempt against him in 1969. Had the coup been successful it could have spelt the end of Noriega's military career, and he undoubtedly vacillated in the early stages. As it turned out, Noriega

Former CIA director George Bush went to great lengths to hide his previous friendly relations with Noriega

backed the winner, and now the sky was the limit. However, the more Noriega's power grew, the more his fellow officers came to fear him. Torrijos himself, who happily used Noriega to do his dirty work, also feared him as amoral and self-seeking (as he confessed to his cousin, Roberto Díaz Herrera). But he preferred to have Noriega on his side rather than working against him, and in 1970 Torrijos appointed him to head the National Guard intelligence branch, G2. The kid from the slums had become the J Edgar Hoover of Panama, and he used his new position to build up files on friend and foe alike.

As head of G2, Lieutenant Colonel Noriega was the official liaison officer between the Panamanian military and all branches of US intelligence. This enormously improved his status as an 'asset' from that of occasional informant to paid agent — and well-paid at that. The US government has gone to great lengths to conceal the amount of money that it paid to the future dictator in the course of his career, but President Carter's CIA chief, Admiral Stansfield Turner, revealed that the Agency was giving Noriega $110,000 a year before he took him off the payroll in 1977. Turner added that after Ronald Reagan came to power in 1981, new Vice-President George Bush insisted on re-hiring Noriega. This kind of money might buy some people's unconditional loyalty, but Noriega saw it as simply a fee for services rendered. He felt quite free to provide similar services to opponents of the US, and indeed to subvert his paymasters' plans whenever it suited his political or personal aims.

Clear evidence emerged in the 1970s and 1980s that Noriega was trafficking guns to the left-wing Sandinista guerrillas in Nicaragua and their counterparts in El Salvador, the FMLN. He did the same favour for the M-19 insurgents in Colombia. It was around this time that State Department officials took to referring to Noriega as 'rent-a-colonel'.

Noriega also turned the tables by recruiting several US soldiers who supplied him with transcripts of US bugging operations on the Panamanian leadership, and even with top-secret National Security Agency documents. The so-called 'Singing Sergeants' affair was hushed up with the compliance of the then CIA director, George Bush, who subsequently exhibited symptoms of chronic amnesia when asked what he knew about Noriega and when he had found out.

Bush and Noriega

Nothing about Bush's relationship with Noriega has ever been easy to pin down. When the US indicted Noriega [in 1988] for drug trafficking, Bush denied having previously known of his dirty business. But in a recent interview, Bush's national security adviser Donald Gregg, in an apparent slip-up, told us that a new CIA study — one not released to the public — traces the drug allegations against the Panamanian general back to the mid-1970s. Indeed, said Gregg, Bush as CIA director had met with Noriega in 1976 and had approved continued US intelligence co-operation with him, despite 'allegations' already linking him to the narcotics trade.

This was the first confirmation from any official source that Bush had a direct role in forging US ties to Noriega.

Gregg was adamant in saying that none of these early drug allegations was 'firm'. But he acknowledged that Panama's defence forces soon became so immersed in drug trafficking that by 1983 Noriega was losing his 'value' to the CIA as an intelligence source. The date is significant: it was in late 1983 that Bush, supposedly on a ceremonial visit, met Noriega in Panama and the Israeli supply network [to the Nicaraguan contras] picked up steam.

It was also during this period that Bush apparently turned to Noriega for a political favour. As [José] Blandón tells it, when US forces invaded Grenada in October of that year, Bush contacted Noriega and asked him to appeal to Fidel Castro not to interfere. Bush staffers now challenge this story, but their objections seem to hinge on a technicality — whether the vice-president made the call himself or had one of his aides do it.

If Noriega was merely 'suspect' to the administration in 1983, the last trappings of innocence fell away from him soon afterward. Former State Department intelligence deputy director Francis McNeil said that by 1984 there was 'hard' evidence of official Panamanian complicity in drug trafficking. A year later, on December 16, 1985, the US ambassador to Panama, Everett Briggs, showed up at the White House to brief the vice-president on the situation. Bush's office now says that the briefing dealt chiefly with illicit money laundering, not the drug trade. But a note by Bush aide Colonel Sam Watson on his daily recorder ... mentions 'narcotics' in reference to the meeting. (Briggs, now ambassador to Honduras, will say only that he provided no 'evidence' of Noriega drug trafficking at the meeting.)

In the summer of 1986, a *New York Times* exposé detonated the few remaining illusions about Noriega's drug activities, as well as his role in US covert operations. In the meantime, reports of contra drug trafficking had so proliferated that they were now, according to newly released [Oliver] North diaries, an abiding preoccupation of the NSC's [National Security Council] contra cheering section.

One North entry, dated mid-1985, remarks that $14 million used to set up the arms 'supermarket' in Honduras 'came from drugs', and cables filed coincidentally by US embassy officials in Costa Rica and letters written by North's 'courier', Rob Owen, link several contra leaders and even a contra cargo plane to illegal drug deliveries.

How so many worthies could have known so much about the contra drug taint — and Bush have known so little — remains unexplained, unless he simply opted not to know.

Latin America Weekly, 14-20 October 1988

Noriega's first contact with the Cuban regime arose out of Washington's request for Panama to help in negotiating the release of an anti-Castro militant who had operated out of Miami. The mission eventually succeeded, even though Panama had no diplomatic relations with Cuba at the time. Torrijos restored these to put pressure on the US during the canal treaty negotiations.

The relationship developed, not least because the Cubans needed Panama to help circumvent the US trade embargo, and both sides were interested in setting up an arms conduit to the Sandinistas. The Torrijos regime, with its left-wing leanings and simultaneous dependence on the US, was a perfect political and ideological crossroads in the Caribbean — and Noriega was the man in the best position to take advantage of it — not only because of his job as intelligence chief but because Torrijos used him as go-between with

Fidel Castro. Hence the paradox that one of the highest-paid US intelligence assets in Latin America ended up being overthrown by a US invasion, accompanied by Cuban and Nicaraguan protests.

Noriega was thus well-placed when Torrijos was killed. Although he could not automatically succeed the 'maximum leader' — that privilege went by seniority to Colonel Florencio Flórez — he and two other senior officers below Flórez began plotting to take over the National Guard almost before Torrijos was cold in his grave.

The other two were Díaz Herrera, executive secretary to the general staff and chief of staff Rubén Darío Paredes, the most senior of the three. They struck a deal to remove Flórez and share power by each taking his turn as GN commander. They persuaded Flórez to step down on 3 March 1982, and Paredes replaced him. The agreement called for Paredes to resign after a year and become the official candidate in the 1984 election, supported by the National Guard.

All went smoothly, until Paredes found he had been hoodwinked and would not, after all, be the candidate. Deprived of his only power base, he could only fume, while Noriega assumed real power as commander of the GN.

The only remaining obstacle to Noriega's ambitions was Díaz Herrera, who was due to take over command in 1989. Noriega duly reneged on the bargain, but even he could scarcely have foreseen how great a part his betrayal of Díaz Herrera would play in his eventual downfall.

The Panama Connection

'General Noriega provides the best example in recent US foreign policy of how a foreign leader is able to manipulate the US to the detriment of our own interests.'

Report of the Subcommittee on Terrorism, Narcotics and International Operations of the Committee on Foreign Relations of the US Senate (Chair: Senator John Kerry).

Given the geographical location of Panama and its status as a haven for funds derived from shady deals, it was only a matter of time before a man like Noriega latched on to the money-making possibilities arising out of drug trafficking.

It is hard to establish precisely when he first became involved with drugs, but the US authorities knew that their man in Panama was a trafficker at least as early as late 1971. According to John Bacon, a former senior agent with the Drug Enforcement Administration

(DEA), the DEA compiled sufficient evidence for an indictment that year, based on information from two Cuban exile fishermen in Miami. The fishermen helped the DEA seize a boatload of marijuana from Panama. According to Bacon:

'After the marihuana was loaded a Panamanian official came aboard. He was introduced to the two Cuban fishermen as Manuel Noriega. He was given a sum of money and the person who made the arrangements said that he [Noriega] was the Panamanian official who made possible the shipment without interference from the Panamanian authorities.'

The US Attorney's office in Miami, however, decided not to proceed with an indictment.

By this time the DEA knew that contacts were developing between Panamanian officials and drug traffickers. In 1972, the US indicted Moisés Torrijos, brother of the Panamanian leader, on heroin charges, but the indictment was not made public and Washington asked Torrijos to curb his brother's activities. This violated US law, which forbids those concerned from disclosing details of an ongoing investigation. During the Nixon years the level of concern at Noriega's activities became so great that, according to a Senate Intelligence Committee report, a drug enforcement official suggested assassination. The idea was quashed by the then head of the Bureau of Narcotics and Dangerous Drugs (precursor of the DEA), John Ingersoll.

From 1977 the newly-elected President Carter gave top priority to signing and ratifying the 1977 Canal Treaties. Congressional opponents of the treaty legislation were looking for any means of derailing it, and evidence of drug trafficking was ideal for the purpose. John Bacon recalls that he was instructed to gather all relevant information from anywhere within the DEA and have it transferred to the Justice Department:

'The purpose was to get any information on Noriega and Panama as a country important in drug trafficking into the US, and to have all of this information removed from DEA files and unavailable.

This attitude set the pattern for the next ten years, in which Noriega — doubtless convinced that he was too valuable to the US government for a little thing like drugs to come between them — vastly increased his involvement, and his take, from the narcotics trade.

Closed-door hearings in the US Senate in 1978 (as part of the treaty ratification process) discussed allegations of drug trafficking by Panamanian officers. Heavily edited transcripts appeared in the media which included references to Noriega himself. At this point a good deal of evidence pointed to his involvement in trafficking, whether or not it was sufficient for an indictment. However, the US authorities had clearly taken a decision not to proceed against him, both because of his value to General Torrijos (and hence to the treaty process) and because, paradoxically, he was co-operating with the DEA.

In reorganising and expanding the National Guard (and renaming it the Defence Forces) in 1983, Noriega also ensured that he had control over all the agencies responsible for drug enforcement — customs, immigration, and port and airport authorities. He also took control of the National Bank of Panama and the Attorney-General's office. In doing so he turned the country's public institutions into branches of a criminal enterprise: not only could he determine who could break the law, he could also offer almost unlimited money-laundering facilities.

This system also enabled Noriega to co-operate selectively with US law enforcement, giving them enough information on rival drug operations, or those deemed expendable, to keep them happy. In yet another irony, the man appointed by Noriega as his chief liaison with the DEA, Inspector Luis Quiel, also acted as an intermediary between the general and the Medellín cartel, the world's premier cocaine traffickers.

Washington's collaboration with Noriega was extremely counter-productive. According to the Kerry Report (quoting a convicted drug smuggler), 'Noriega's close relationship with the DEA allowed [his partners] to advise other drug smugglers about whether or not their planes were on a DEA watch list.'

Today DEA officials are acutely embarrassed that until shortly before his indictment on drug charges they regularly sent Noriega letters praising his co-operation, a type of document known in the business as an 'attaboy'. According to the head of the DEA, John Lawn — the signatory on many of them —'these were not character references' but praise for specific operations in which the FDP's assistance had been vital. An examination of specific letters suggests the reverse.

In May 1986 Lawn wrote to Noriega of the DEA's 'deep appreciation for the vigorous anti-drug trafficking policy that you have adopted, which is reflected in the numerous expulsions from Panama of accused traffickers...' As late as May 1987 he wrote that the 'DEA has long welcomed our close association and we stand ready to proceed jointly against international drug traffickers whenever the opportunity arises.' In April 1987 even the International Police Organisation (Interpol) presented Noriega with its medal of honour for his contribution to the struggle against terrorism and drug trafficking.

General Manuel Antonio Noriega   (Carlos Reyes, ANDES Press Agency)

The letters indicate that the DEA (like other US agencies) was turning a blind eye to evidence of massive law-breaking in order to take advantage of selective co-operation by the criminals themselves. In order to beef up their arrest and seizure statistics, they became in effect accessories to the smuggling of huge quantities of cocaine into the US market, at a time when the prevention of this trade was supposed to be among Washington's top priorities.

In June 1986 an article appeared in the *New York Times*, written by Seymour Hersh and entitled 'Panama Strongman Said to Trade in Drugs, Arms and Illicit Money'. Although long aware of Noriega's drugs links, the State Department feigned surprise and commissioned an investigation which, according to one official, concluded that

'Noriega has to know [about the drug trafficking] and is likely getting a share.'

Washington shelved the issue on this occasion to ensure Noriega's co-operation on Nicaragua. In 1986 Colonel Oliver North's illegal activities in support of the Nicaraguan contras were at their height, and Panama appeared an essential ally. The US government has acknowledged at least one significant contribution to the contra cause by Noriega: he sent a sum of $100,000 to their Southern Front in July 1984. Precise details of the North-Noriega relationship remain closely guarded.

According to the man who later became the key witness in the case against Noriega — his personal pilot, Floyd Carlton — the general had been involved with the Medellín cartel almost since its inception in 1981 as an organised group. Outright collaboration began in 1982, and Noriega immediately began to see substantial rewards:

> '. .. Noriega was paid $100,000 for Carlton's first flight, $150,000 for Carlton's second flight, $200,000 for Carlton's third flight of cocaine and $250,000 for Carlton's fourth flight of cocaine.' (Kerry Report)

In May 1984, the FDP raided a massive cocaine laboratory in the Darién jungle on the border with Colombia. According to testimony by Noriega's former adviser José Blandón, the cartel had paid the general $5 million to protect this plant, but he had come under pressure from the DEA to take some action. Blandón further alleges that only Fidel Castro's mediation prevented the cartel from ordering Noriega's assassination on this occasion.

However, it was in Blandón's interests to testify against Noriega, and many of his claims have since been discredited, notably by John Dinges in his book *Our Man in Panama*. Dinges revealed that 'a significant number of [Blandón's] allegations defy confirmation and in some cases [they] are implausible or demonstrably false.' He claimed that the Darién laboratory story fell into this category.

Disagreement also exists over the amount of money Noriega earned from drug trafficking (as distinct from his other corrupt activities). Washington has put Noriega's total wealth at $300 million, but it has provided no evidence for this and has so far only traced a fraction of that amount. After it invaded Panama, the US seized $5.8 million in cash from his house and froze around $20 million in overseas bank accounts on the grounds that it was drug money. However, Washington backed down when the judge in the case ordered the prosecution to prove this. Rather than give the defence a preview of its case (or perhaps because it could not prove the point), the US government authorised the release of part of Noriega's assets. Dinges argued that Noriega's drugs earnings totalled $10-15 million, making him 'a mid-level player'. He added that 'the evidence suggests that Noriega participated in major drug activity for only a two-to-three year period in the early 1980s and then became a trusted and overtly zealous DEA collaborator.'

Whatever the extent of Noriega's involvement with trafficking, he was undoubtedly receiving mixed signals from the US over its acceptability, right up to the date of his indictment. Even while the 'Department of State was attempting to distance itself from Noriega, the Department of Defense and CIA were simultaneously sending him encouraging signals.' (Kerry Report).

As a former National Security Council member, Norman Bailey, put it:

'Clear and incontrovertible evidence was, at best, ignored and, at worst, hidden and denied by many different agencies and departments of the Government of the US in such a way as to provide cover and protection for [Noriega's] activities while, at the same time, assuring that they did maximum damage to those very interests that the officials involved were sworn to uphold and defend.'

Beginning of the End

In early 1987 everything looked good for Noriega. He had been in sole command of the FDP for four years, his civilian opponents were weak and divided and there seemed every chance that a corrupt and fraudulent electoral process would deliver his candidate (maybe even Noriega himself) a fresh presidential mandate in elections scheduled for 1989.

The ambitions of his putative successor as FDP commander, chief of staff Colonel Roberto Díaz Herrera, must have seemed a relatively minor inconvenience to a man like Noriega at the height of his power. Yet Díaz Herrera was to play a crucial role in a chain of events which eventually brought Noriega's regime to an end.

Under the terms of the 1983 agreement Díaz Herrera was to take over the job of FDP commander in 1989. But by mid-1987 it was obvious that Noriega had no intention of turning over the post. Díaz Herrera was chief of staff, the number two FDP position, but he felt increasingly marginalised from decision-making. Eventually, on 25 May 1987, Noriega informed Díaz Herrera that he was to be retired.

Middle-class protester holds up a $10 bill stamped with the words "Narcotrafficker Manuel Antonio Noriega". The opposition soon faded away, after it failed to involve trade unions and the poor. (SIPA/Rex Features)

Noriega and Díaz Herrera agreed a retirement package including a pre-retirement promotion to general and a lucrative overseas posting, but Noriega once more reneged on the deal. Díaz Herrera retaliated with the only weapon he had — detailed information on Noriega's misdeeds. In a series of interviews and press conferences, he accused Noriega of the 1984 election fraud, of the 1985 murder of the well-known opposition figure Hugo Spadafora, and of responsibility (with the CIA) for Omar Torrijos' death in 1981. However, Díaz Herrera said he had no evidence that Noriega was involved in drug trafficking.

The statements, though scarcely revelations to a nation which had known or suspected as much for years, galvanised the opposition to Noriega. Thousands took to the streets in spontaneous demonstrations which lasted for a week. The opposition formed a Civic Crusade for Justice and Democracy (*Cruzada Civilista*), which the regime greeted with riot squads, tear gas and the suspension of constitutional rights. The Civic Crusade revolved around the Chamber of Commerce and comprised some 200 professional, business and civic organisations, supported by the opposition political parties.

Its members included organisations like the Rotary Club, the Scouts Association and bodies representing dentists, insurance brokers and restaurateurs. Most of the protesters were white and middle class. They turned up, as PJ O'Rourke wrote in *Rolling Stone* magazine, 'in nice ties and linen dirndl skirts . . . in BMWs and Jeep Wagoneers . . .' Foreign journalists joked that the numbers turning out to demonstrate depended on the available parking space.

The labour movement was almost entirely absent. It had been co-opted and then neutralised by the military regime. As Raúl Leis, director of the Panamanian Centre for Research and Social Action (CEASPA), wrote after the invasion, 'the process initiated by Torrijos and brought to a close by the invasion was characterized by a profound distrust of autonomous organizing by the poor. Demobilization and the co-optation [sic] and corruption of leaders were the result.'

The Role of the Church

Although most Panamanians are at least nominally Catholic, the Church played a much less prominent role in the 1987-89 conflict than it has done in countries like El Salvador and Nicaragua in recent years. Nonetheless the Church hierarchy, led by Archbishop Marcos McGrath, supported the opposition at certain key moments.

After Colonel Díaz Herrera's first public accusations against Noriega, the archbishop sent several priests to stay at Díaz Herrera's house in an attempt to provide a measure of protection. On 1 November 1987 the Church called on all officers who had passed normal retirement age to step down; a move which would have meant the resignation of Noriega and many of his closest allies.

When the crisis worsened, and Noriega ousted Erick Arturo Delvalle from the presidency, the Church demanded the restoration of human rights, an end to restrictions on the opposition press, and the 'full and effective subordination of military forces to civilian authority'. It also offered to mediate, but although acting President Manuel Solís Palma accepted the proposal, the Civic Crusade declined to talk unless Noriega stepped down.

Archbishop McGrath also demanded that the US end its campaign of economic sanctions, which he said was threatening the life of the Panamanian people, and stressed the need for a Panamanian solution, without outside interference.

After the electoral fraud of May 1989 the Church sided even more openly with the opposition, calling 'in the name of God [for] those ultimately responsible [to] respect the will of the people'. The offer of mediation was repeated, but with ADOC leaders standing beside McGrath as he described the regime as repressive and illegitimate, it seemed unlikely to be taken up.

Noriega personally disliked McGrath, who had sought to keep the Church independent of the FDP. The Church's weakness as an institution also limited the bishops' role: only about one in five of Panamanian Catholics are active worshippers, and three quarters of the clergy are foreign. As relations deteriorated in 1989, the government-controlled media called for the expulsion of foreign priests.

Finally, the Church was itself divided, as elsewhere in Central America, between traditionalists and supporters of the so-called 'popular Church'; while some priests, whether through opportunism or conviction, remained loyal to the regime.

As noted earlier, the labour movement reached its apogee during the early Torrijos years, before a resurgent business class pushed it back. Law 95 of 1976 revised the progressive labour code: it curtailed the right to strike, introduced a wage freeze and undermined job security. The unions then regrouped to recoup some of what they had lost, and Law 95 was partially revised. A new, independent labour federation (CATI) appeared in response to the inaction of some union leaders.

However, organised labour's exclusion from the growth areas of the economy, such as the Colón Free Zone and the financial centre, blocked the growth of the unions, and by the late 1980s only 17 per cent of the workforce was unionised. Almost all unions refused to join the Crusade and labour in general remained relatively passive in the absence of any non-governmental movement promoting a genuinely nationalist position. The unions largely ignored the Crusade's strike calls and if anything tended to line up with the regime against the pro-US business groups.

The poor and the working class found it hard to identify with the pale-skinned, European-blooded business leaders whose grip on government power had been prised away in 1968. The *rabiblancos* had little appeal for those whose sense of pride in their nation, though now a little dented, derived from the Torrijos years and the struggle for the canal. Arnulfo Arias was the only politician capable of bridging that gap, but his *Panameñista* movement was badly divided and losing ground to its rivals.

Noriega made good use of his dark skin and humble origins, as well as of the Torrijos legacy, despite his own total lack of progressive credentials. A US Senate resolution calling for the removal of Noriega and other senior officials pending an investigation of the Díaz Herrera charges merely played into the dictator's hands. Now he could portray the opposition as mere tools of the US, partners in a plot to keep the canal in US hands.

The Murder of Hugo Spadafora

Prior to June 1987, the opposition to Noriega was confused and divided. It was characterised by a lack of leadership and an almost complete dearth of heroes. It is significant that the catalyst for the events of 1987-89 was provided by an FDP officer, Díaz Herrera, whose downfall had initially been welcomed by the opposition.

The only popular hero in the anti-Noriega pantheon (with the qualified exception of Arnulfo Arias) was a man who represented the antithesis of almost everything the Crusade leaders stood for, and whose outspoken opposition cost him his life.

Hugo Spadafora was a handsome embodiment of revolutionary romanticism. A doctor who had fought against the Portuguese colonialists in Guinea Bissau, and then on the side of the Sandinistas against the Somoza dictatorship, he was a believer in the spirit of *torrijismo*. After joining the underground opposition to Torrijos in 1968, he had been won over and had become deputy health minister.

A close friend of leading Sandinista Edén Pastora, Spadafora joined the former 'Commander Zero' when he launched his own contra campaign against his former comrades. Later, however, he broke with Pastora and began to turn his attention to the man he believed had betrayed the ideals of *torrijismo*, Manuel Antonio Noriega.

In June 1982, even before Noriega took command of the National Guard/FDP, Spadafora publicly attacked him for repressing the opposition, and even stated that he had information about Noriega's involvement in drug trafficking. No one in the opposition had ever dared to be so direct, and Spadafora had only his reputation to protect him. In the end it was not enough.

Over the next three years he gathered information on corruption, gun-running and drug dealing. Occasionally he would return to the attack, always in the most direct language. Noriega made it clear that he could expect to pay a heavy price, but Spadafora was not deterred. In an interview in the opposition newspaper *La Prensa* in September 1984 he declared that 'the day they don't allow me to enter and circulate freely in my country, that will be the day I enter at the head of a guerrilla force.'

His prediction was wide of the mark. The day came almost exactly a year later. Spadafora was pulled off a bus by FDP soldiers just inside the northern border. The following morning his decapitated body was found, stuffed into a green canvas mailbag, a few hundred yards inside Costa Rica.

It was a rare (though not unique) instance of political murder by the military regime, and profoundly shocking to ordinary Panamanians, who had little doubt that Noriega had ordered it, even though he was out of the country at the time. In one act, Noriega had destroyed much of his credibility as the successor to Torrijos, for in killing Spadafora the regime had attacked the embodiment of *torrijismo*.

The ripples from the murder continued to spread in the months that followed. Díaz Herrera, who had been left in command and who seems to have been ignorant of the plot, never forgave Noriega for leaving him to clear up the mess. President Nicolás Ardito Barletta announced a full investigation, and was forced to resign less than two weeks after the murder, causing a cooling of relations with Washington, which froze $50 million in aid money. The pictures of Spadafora's mutilated corpse convinced US Senator Jesse Helms to convene investigative hearings on Panama. Like Banquo's ghost, Spadafora would return again and again to haunt Noriega.

President Erick Arturo Delvalle seemed determined to do Noriega's bidding and avoid Ardito Barletta's fate. On 11 June he imposed a state of emergency, suspending nine articles of the constitution, and banned demonstrations in response to an opposition call for a general strike. He denied Díaz Herrera's accusations and rejected calls for political change. After demonstrators, organised by the FDP, threw rocks at the US embassy and destroyed embassy employees' cars, Delvalle told the ambassador to send the bill to the US Senate because their resolution had caused the riot.

Washington cut military and economic aid, and the CIA finally took Noriega off its payroll. But over the next few months, faced with birdshot, teargas, beatings and imprisonment, the opposition demonstrators gradually ran out of steam. By October it seemed as if Noriega had restored his grip on power. He had muzzled the opposition press, arrested Díaz Herrera and forced the main Crusade leaders into exile. The economy was in turmoil, but Noriega's resolve was unblunted. The protracted humiliation of US policymakers had begun.

Washington Turns on a Client

By the mid-1980s Manuel Noriega had served governments of the US for 20 years as perhaps their most useful agent in the western hemisphere (and certainly the highest-ranking in terms of the office he held in his own country). After recruiting, training and bestowing honours upon him, the US government turned on Noriega and launched a campaign to remove him from power, regardless of the cost to Panama.

In July 1987 the Reagan administration embarked upon a policy of economic sanctions against Panama, beginning with the suspension of aid, a gesture more symbolic than harmful. In December that year it suspended Panama's sugar quota, an equally minor step, but one which hurt President Delvalle, who had built his fortune on sugar. Washington also instructed its representatives at the multilateral funding bodies to vote against loans to the country. In the interim, the White House initiated the first of many attempts to negotiate Noriega's exit from Panama.

At the end of 1987, after much prevarication (Noriega proved to be a master at playing for time) the US abandoned what came to be called the Blandón Plan for the dictator's graceful exit.

The confrontation reached the point of no return when in February 1988 it was announced that two Florida grand juries had indicted Noriega for drug offences. The timing was partly coincidental and owed more to the ambitions of the local US attorneys than to any grand design. But by the time the indictments were ready it was impossible for the government to block them without causing a political storm. A meeting chaired by Deputy National Security Adviser John D Negroponte reviewed the situation and declined to recommend intervention in the case, despite the misgivings of some of those present.

The Blandón Plan

José Blandón was serving in 1987 as Panamanian consul in New York. It was a post he had been given the year before, when Noriega had forced Delvalle to remove from the cabinet and his inner circle a number of officials — including Blandón — who were regarded as less than wholeheartedly loyal to the general.

As a close adviser to Delvalle, and a long-standing, senior member of the ruling Democratic Revolutionary Party (PRD), Blandón was an insider. At first it appeared that his manoeuvres in New York had the blessing of Noriega, but as the divide between the dictator and his supposedly compliant president grew, it is clear that Blandón came down on the side of Delvalle.

In late August 1987 the consul began his attempts to obtain agreement on a plan which, in essence, involved trading the departure of Noriega for an agreement by the Reagan administration to grant him immunity from prosecution. The target date for his stepping down was April 1988. It also contemplated the installation of a transitional, power-sharing government with the opposition, pending elections which would mark the end of military rule.

The plan foundered when someone (possibly a Pentagon official) sent Noriega a draft he was not intended to see. Blandón was fired, and his only remaining card was his insider's knowledge of the general. Even this was not enough of a threat, however, to convince Noriega to step down, and a further series of bungled US attempts to deliver a tough message left him even more convinced that he could survive the crisis.

Having failed to negotiate the general's removal, and now committed to his criminal prosecution, the Reagan administration embarked on another tactic. In this new phase President Delvalle played a central role. After a Miami meeting with US Assistant Secretary of State Elliott Abrams, Delvalle returned to Panama and announced Noriega's resignation as head of the Defence Forces. The general refused even to talk to him, and an emergency meeting of the Panamanian legislature swiftly sacked Delvalle and replaced him with Education Minister Manuel Solís Palma, who took the title of minister in charge of the presidency. Delvalle thus became the fourth president in six years to be ousted by the military.

In a move which defied all logic for a campaign ostensibly aimed at restoring democracy to Panama, the US then announced that it would continue to regard Delvalle as the legitimate head of state. Delvalle had been elected vice-president in a fraudulent poll and achieved the presidency itself via a military coup. Of all the US allies, only El Salvador followed Washington's lead. The Panamanian opposition, which regarded Delvalle as a class traitor and a time-server, only agreed to back his 'provisional government of national reconciliation' in exchange for US guarantees that this would mean the end of Noriega. A member of the Civic Crusade acknowledged that 'the US had laid down as a non-negotiable condition our support for the constitutionality symbolised by Delvalle.'

This single policy decision, perhaps more than any other in the final two years of the Noriega regime, revealed the hollowness of US claims to be supporting the interests of the people of Panama. Delvalle had put his name to decrees suspending their rights, had congratulated Noriega on FDP suppression of demonstrations and defended him against charges he knew to be accurate. He had called US sanctions 'imperialist aggression'. His personal support did not even extend to all the members of his own family; yet to Washington he embodied Panamanian sovereignty.

In March 1988, officers critical of his leadership launched a coup attempt against Noriega. Their leader, Major Fernando Quezada, was encouraged — though given little practical assistance — by Southcom. The coup failed: the rebels did not fire a single shot and were outmanoeuvred in a couple of hours. Far from posing a danger to Noriega the move enabled him to identify and remove dissident officers. Major Quezada eventually got his reward when he was named head of the new Public Force in August 1990, but it was a short-lived triumph. For the time being at least, Washington had lost the option of an 'inside job' and with negotiations also at a standstill the US concentrated on trying to bring down the regime with economic sanctions.

Understanding the U-Turn

Many explanations have been put forward as to why Washington turned so aggressively against its former client. First, there is the official argument that US policy towards Noriega changed because of his criminal activities (trafficking in drugs, murder, election-rigging and commerce in intelligence and prohibited technology with Cuba and Eastern Europe).

But many other heads of government in Latin America and elsewhere engage in these same activities — though perhaps with less diversification than Manuel Noriega — and no US government representative has adequately explained why Noriega should have been singled out for punishment. Moreover, Washington knew of his activities long before it chose to rid Panama of Noriega. The involvement in drug trafficking had been apparent for almost 20 years; the US embassy possessed documentary evidence of election-rigging in 1984; the most significant murder — that of Hugo Spadafora — dated back to 1985, with immediate, credible accusations of military involvement.

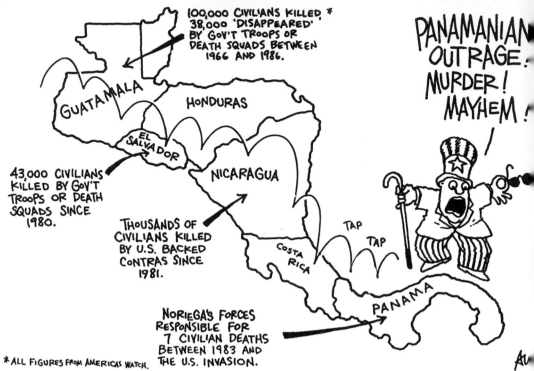

100,000 CIVILIANS KILLED *
38,000 'DISAPPEARED'
BY GOV'T TROOPS OR
DEATH SQUADS BETWEEN
1966 AND 1986.

PANAMANIAN OUTRAGE: MURDER! MAYHEM!

GUATAMALA

HONDURAS

EL SALVADOR

NICARAGUA

43,000 CIVILIANS
KILLED BY GOV'T
TROOPS OR DEATH
SQUADS SINCE
1980.

THOUSANDS OF
CIVILIANS KILLED
BY U.S. BACKED
CONTRAS SINCE
1981.

COSTA RICA

TAP

TAP

PANAMA

NORIEGA'S FORCES
RESPONSIBLE FOR
7 CIVILIAN DEATHS
BETWEEN 1983 AND
THE U.S. INVASION.

* ALL FIGURES FROM AMERICAS WATCH.

A US cartoonist's view of Washington's double standards on human rights

There had been high-level discussions on how to deal with Noriega under every US administration since that of Richard Nixon in the early 1970s. Each administration had decided to conceal the facts rather than press for criminal proceedings, and the argument — in essence — was always the same. Washington needed Noriega, whether as an intelligence asset, a key player in the canal treaties process, or a leader who could provide facilities vital to the illegal US war on Nicaragua.

Noriega's own explanation, favoured by many nationalists in Panama and elsewhere in Latin America, was that Washington decided to move against him in order to renege on the 1977 treaties and retain control of the canal beyond the year 2000. This would require the election in May 1989 of a Panamanian government subservient to US interests, and this in turn would mean the prior removal of the general.

Particularly crucial — runs the argument — would be the continued presence of US military bases after the year 2000, when the treaties require their removal. The invasion had to occur in December because the Canal Treaties require that a Panamanian take over as head of the Canal Commission on 1 January 1990 (which may be why the invasion was originally planned for that date).

The past history of US-Panamanian relations made such a theory highly plausible, and some evidence for it existed. On 23 October 1986 (as Ricardo Arias Calderón noted in his *Foreign Affairs* article), US ambassador Arthur Davis delivered a speech in Panama in which he hinted at a link between the transfer of the canal and domestic political changes:

> 'Fully functioning democratic institutions in Panama [he said] are the best guarantee to Americans and Panamanians alike for success in the turnover of the canal to Panama.'

There were many US politicians in the late 1980s who favoured maintaining US control over the canal indefinitely, and some of these (such as Senator Jesse Helms) became involved in the campaign to get rid of Noriega. Ronald Reagan himself had led the attack on the Torrijos-Carter treaties during the 1980 presidential campaign.

The Santa Fé II Committee, a think tank on the Republican right, recommended in 1988 that, once a democratic regime existed in Panama:

> 'discussions must begin on a realistic defense of the canal after the year 2000. Those talks should include the US' retention of limited facilities in Panama (principally Howard airbase and Rodman Naval Base), for proper force projection in the western hemisphere.'

A campaign against Noriega, however, was not necessary to achieve this particular end. Unlike his predecessor Omar Torrijos, Noriega was a pragmatist and an opportunist rather than an idealist. He played the 'canal card' in response to US pressure rather than through any deeply-felt nationalism or 'third worldist' position. He had previously co-operated with the US Defense Department, allowing the largest joint military exercises ever held in Panama to take place in the three years prior to 1987. Washington could no doubt have induced him to concede military base rights beyond the year 2000. Significantly, both the Pentagon and the CIA were notoriously slow to accept that he would have to go.

While both explanations for the sudden U-turn are superficially plausible, neither is wholly convincing. When great events occur, such as military invasions, the natural tendency is to attribute to them coherent motivations and grand design. This is all the more tempting when, as in the case of Panama, the event occurs at the end of a two-and-a-half year escalation of pressure by an aggressor. But Operation Just Cause resulted more from blunders and miscalculations than grand design. Two administrations embarked upon the venture believing that Noriega's overthrow would prove a relatively easy task.

When the initial results proved this false, US policymakers chose to escalate rather than back down.

The forced retirement in June 1987 of Colonel Roberto Díaz Herrera, Noriega's heir-apparent, provided the catalyst for the sudden policy change. Washington saw Díaz Herrera, a cousin of Torrijos, as a 'leftist', and may have feared he would assume control of the government, with an anti-American foreign policy, were Noriega to fall. By ousting him, Noriega unwittingly removed an obstacle to his own overthrow.

Whether or not this was a factor, Díaz Herrera's accusations against Noriega made his crimes much harder to ignore and led immediately to internal unrest in Panama on an almost unprecedented scale. Above all, US Panama policy aimed to ensure stability, and once Noriega had become a destabilising factor his removal became much easier to contemplate. Having disposed of the argument that Noriega was vital to US interests because any other alternative would be worse, the logjam was broken. Now all the factors which had caused serious concern to previous administrations came flooding back to the surface, and the logical answer was to remove the general.

Coincidences helped to hasten the end. One of Noriega's main supporters in Washington was CIA director William Casey; but Casey had fallen seriously ill at the time of the Iran-contra revelations the previous autumn, and he died just as Díaz Herrera's revelations were hitting the press. The Iran-contra hearings themselves provided a certain motivation for the Reagan administration to distance itself from sleazy allies in Central America. The administration also knew that the Florida drug indictments against Noriega were nearing a conclusion, and that it would be hard to block them.

A more baffling question is why both the Reagan and Bush administrations chose to make the removal of Noriega a high-profile test of machismo, rather than opting for 'quiet diplomacy'. The answer seems to lie in the historical relationship between the US and Latin America, and in particular that between the US and Panama.

Put bluntly, most US policymakers found it hard to believe that a 'tin-pot dictator in a banana republic' could withstand sustained US pressure. They failed to understand that international pressure was counter-productive when it came unilaterally from Washington, and thus they inadvertently strengthened Noriega's distinctly dubious credentials as an 'anti-imperialist'.

Questions of Strategy

A significant part of the debate around Washington's true intentions towards Panama hinges on the strategic significance of the canal and the US military bases along its banks. Different individuals see these as either pivotal to US security and economic well-being, or as optional extras to which several alternatives could be found.

In the 1980s the canal accounted for about 5 per cent of worldwide ocean-going trade and handled an average 13,000 ships a year, but its importance to some countries, especially in Latin America, was much greater than the percentage figure would suggest. More than half the trade of Ecuador and of some Central American nations went through the canal, and Chile and Peru both depended on it for around 40 per cent of their foreign commerce.

The canal was much less significant to the US in terms of total trade, even though nearly three quarters of the traffic passing through the

The Pharaoh's Legacy

In the annals of Empires there is no artifact more charged with passion and purpose than a canal, for great works of irrigation and navigation were always hallmarks of imperial grandeur, and sometimes its excuses too. Wherever Emperors ruled in foreign parts, they commemorated themselves with mighty waterworks, as though to demonstrate their mastery not merely over the lesser breeds, but over nature herself. In Mesopotamia the rulers of Babylon brought the desert to life; in Egypt the Pharaohs linked the Mediterranean with the Indian Ocean; grand aqueducts marked the progress of Rome across Europe; in India the Victorians summoned new provinces into existence by their monumental dams and conduits. The Suez Canal, though the British did not actually build it, became so inescapable an emblem of their imperialism that the phrase 'East of Suez' was a synonym for Empire itself, and the Empire's desperate attempt to keep control of the waterway became in the end its bitter curtain call. Nearly always the constructions were destined to outlive their sponsoring sovereignties, and when all the substance of command had faded, the drums were silenced with the rhetoric, then the great work lingered on, crumbling more slowly down the centuries, like the last ironic smile of the Cheshire cat.

'An Imperial Specimen', Jan Morris, 1975, from the anthology *Destinations*, OUP, 1982 canal either originated in or was destined for a US port. Less than 10 per cent of US trade is dependent on the canal, although some industries would have suffered substantial disruption if it had been closed for any reason. The biggest volume of traffic was the two-way trade between the US and Asia, especially Japan and South Korea, with US grain and coal exports the major items.

The overall importance of the canal declined throughout the 1980s, and will continue to do so unless improvements are carried out. Modern supertankers and large bulk carriers, representing about 6 per cent of worldwide tonnage, are unable to pass through the 1,000ft-by-110ft locks which were designed (with room to spare) around the dimensions of the liner *Titanic* and the warship *Pennsylvania*, the biggest ships afloat at the turn of the century.

The completion in 1982 of an oil pipeline across Panama took nearly 50 per cent of oil shipments out of the canal, and other alternatives to the waterway were also growing, including greatly improved overland travel across the US. The Canal Commission's own figures showed that most of the major categories of cargo which passed through the canal could find alternative routes.

Although the original lock machinery, first used in 1914, was so well designed that it was perfectly serviceable 80 years later, by the 1980s other bottlenecks limited the volume of traffic through the waterway. There was an urgent need to widen the cut known as Corte Culebra (or Gaillard Cut) between the locks at the Pacific end of the canal and Gatún Lake. This could only take one-way traffic for part of its length; while a two-way passage would increase canal capacity from 42 to 52 ships a day.

Another possibility, under discussion for decades, was the revival of plans for a sea-level canal capable of taking even the biggest vessels. This option particularly attracted the Japanese, much of whose trade is carried in such ships. Although discussions took place, a sea-level canal presented enormous problems. The level of the Pacific is higher than that of the Caribbean and any link between the two would give rise to a strong tide. This in turn would bring Pacific sea life into the Caribbean, with an incalculable ecological impact.

In strategic terms US policymakers have described the canal as a 'choke point' — one of those dots on the map whose control is believed to be vital to US national interests. This view is partly historical: when all the ships in the US navy could pass through the canal it gave the fleet much greater flexibility than would have been the case had they been forced to use the Horn route.

By the late 20th century, however, the US navy ran separate operations in the two oceans, and the number of naval vessels passing through the canal each year fell to around 30 in the 1980s. Even so, at the height of the Vietnam war this figure rose to over 1,500. Specialists also claimed that the canal had a role to play in the relationship between the US and its NATO allies. According to Joe Cirincione of the Carnegie Endowment for International Peace:

'The canal remains important in NATO war plans, which rely on unimpeded access for the rapid transfer of amphibious forces, escorts and destroyers between the Atlantic and Pacific oceans as needed, as well as for trade and movement of raw materials and oil from coast to coast.'

Admittedly, this was written before the collapse of the Warsaw Pact, and at a time of reassessment on the part of strategic planners it is hard to gauge just how crucial the canal will be in the year 2000, when it is due to be taken over by Panama.

Whatever doubts there may have been over the future of the canal, few disputed the importance of the US military bases and the role of Southcom. As the Santa Fé II Committee implied, US 'force projection' in Latin America (in other words, its ability to intervene as and when it chooses) has depended in large measure on the presence in this central location of base facilities, listening devices and intelligence units. Under the treaties, all these had to go by the year 2000, and none of the available alternative sites for Southcom — whether in the southern US or on the territory of a compliant neighbour — offered a comparable location.

In the 1980s, in violation of the Carter-Torrijos treaties (though in many cases with the connivance of the Noriega regime), Southcom played an important role in the guerrilla wars in El Salvador and Nicaragua. It served as the base for spy planes and other forms of intelligence gathering and was even used to train Salvadorean soldiers.

According to US defence plans Southcom would relocate, but this did not necessarily mean that all US bases would be dismantled. The possibility remained that a leasing agreement, such as that which operated in the Philippines, could be signed. Clearly, both the canal and the bases had some strategic importance to the US. The issue, both before and after the invasion, was not so much their exact value but the best way of ensuring their continued use by Washington.

The extreme option would be to refuse to comply with the treaties, and one could scarcely accuse the Panamanians of paranoia if they concluded that this was the underlying objective of the anti-Noriega campaign. Congressional pressure was building, and in his farewell interview before leaving office, President Reagan openly declared that such a course should be considered, especially if Noriega remained in power.

> 'Of course it's too late for me, but I think [renouncing the treaties] is something definitely to look at because our attempts to oust him were in line with the thinking of a great many people in Panama and there is no question about his totalitarianism ... Let me just say that, whatever the situation is, that is something that should be taken into consideration by whoever is in charge at that time.'

Nonetheless, most policymakers appeared to believe that the canal was too vulnerable to sabotage to be effectively defended except through co-operation with the government of Panama. And the bases too depended on the goodwill of the Panamanians: one former head of Southcom, testifying before a congressional committee, advocated relocation on the grounds that it was impossible to run a serious military operation when power and water supplies were controlled by a potentially hostile host.

For Washington in the 1980s the best way to keep the canal bases open was to ensure that the Panamanian government was sympathetic to US interests. By mid-1987 that description could no longer reasonably be applied to General Noriega. Instead Noriega's replacement by his civilian opponents was the best available, short-term option for Washington as 1990 approached. The only outstanding question was, how?

Chapter 4
Failing to Get the General

Between June 1987 and December 1989 Washington tried every available means of ridding itself of its troublesome former ally. Economic sanctions, covert action, direct and indirect negotiations with Noriega, multilateral pressure through the Organization of American States — and finally, unilateral military intervention. The US even seriously considered kidnapping the general in order to bring him to trial in Florida. Often actions intended to weaken Noriega ended up by harming Washington's allies in Panama, and the State Department had to bring political pressure to bear to make them fall into line with actions nominally intended for their benefit.

It is part of the flimsy US justification for Operation Just Cause that all options short of an invasion had been exhausted. The truth is that much of what was tried was in itself illegal under international law, and that hardly any use was made of the extensive regional and worldwide mechanisms for the peaceful resolution of disputes. On several occasions Washington appeared to be deliberately blocking promising attempts at a negotiated solution to the crisis, instead preferring to raise the stakes to such a degree that invasion and massive loss of life was the only remaining path.

Economic Sanctions
The campaign of sanctions against the Noriega regime began with a series of relatively low-key measures in the second half of 1987. The cancellation of military and economic aid was followed by the termination of Panama's US sugar quota and instructions to US representatives on multilateral aid bodies to vote against loans to the

Noriega regime. Though irritating, these served more as warning shots than a concerted effort to sink the Panamanian economy.

It was only after the palace coup against President Delvalle that, in March 1988, Washington brought out the big guns. Even then, it acted in a clumsy and unco-ordinated fashion that helped give Noriega time to work out ways of avoiding the worst effects of the sanctions.

As a first step, the Reagan administration removed Panama from the list of countries receiving preferential trade treatment under the Generalised System of Preferences (GSP) and the Caribbean Basin Initiative (CBI). A complete trade embargo would have been virtually impossible to sustain because of Panama's unique position as a crossroads of world trade. It would also have been illegal under the 1977 Canal Treaties, although it is a moot point whether this would have deterred Washington for long.

Lawyers acting on behalf of President Delvalle, still recognised by the US as the legitimate head of state, succeeded in placing all Panamanian government accounts in the US — amounting to around $40-50 million — under the control of his 'government in exile'. The US then announced that it would put Canal Commission payments (about $7 million a month) into these accounts, rather than remitting them to the Noriega regime.

Not until a month after the Delvalle government filed its lawsuits did the Reagan administration finally invoke the International Emergency Economic Powers Act (the legislation used to impose sanctions on Nicaragua) and formally blocked the Panamanian government's access to its US accounts. It also banned payments (such as taxes and electricity and phone bills) by US citizens and companies to the Noriega government, insisting they be paid into the Delvalle accounts.

Delvalle's 'government' consisted of little more than a name and a bank account but he received $750,000 a month to run it. This expenditure has never been accounted for, although much of it went to support supposedly 'clandestine' operations to overthrow Noriega. The post-invasion government attempted, without success, to impose some retrospective accounting on Delvalle, who is also alleged to have benefited — while president under Noriega — from the usual slush-fund available to the FDP's front-man.

Advertised as devastating, the US measures taken in March and April 1988 posed little danger to the military regime. Washington hoped its much-heralded 'cash strangulation' would weaken the regime by denying Panama access to US dollars. Instead, Noriega simply obtained dollars from a variety of non-US sources. However, US financial pressure proved quite effective in destroying the banking and financial services sector which had been so painstakingly built up during the Torrijos years. Unfortunately this hurt US allies within Panama more than it did Noriega.

To prevent a run on the banks and capital flight, the government ordered them to close, and they remained shut for withdrawals from 4 March to 9 May. Panamanians who did not have dollar accounts abroad were left to manage as best they could with the cash in their pockets. Shops and businesses refused cheques, credit cards and travellers' cheques, and systems of barter and personal vouchers had to be devised to replace cash. The government was forced to delay payments to state sector workers and even the military, encouraging US policymakers to believe that the end was at hand.

By mid-March, for the first time since the crisis began, unionised workers began to appear on the streets. Hospital workers, port workers and others from the public sector went on strike and clashed with police in demonstrations against the delay in receiving their wage packets. Most made it clear, however, that their protests were not linked to those of the Civic Crusade. 'We don't know anything about all that,' said one woman port employee to the Madrid newspaper *El País*. 'What we want is for the government to pay our salaries, and if it doesn't it should go.'

Crowds wielding baseball bats and other weapons attacked supermarkets, and many parents made it clear they preferred to steal rather than see their children go hungry. Large numbers of pensioners staged street protests when they found that they could not cash their fortnightly cheques.

In response, the government cut the budget to the bone and issued emergency decrees suspending rent payment obligations and requiring food manufacturers and distributors to work as usual. To prevent shortages of bread, the government seized two flour mills which had joined a strike organised by the Crusade. Power cuts and water shortages added to the sense of crisis. 'In ten days,' one journalist wrote, 'Panama has turned into Central America.'

Even US officials began to express concern about the impact of sanctions on the Panamanian economy. Treasury Secretary James Baker said the government was worried 'because what we've tried to do is take action that would not hurt the Panamanian people. We don't want to hurt the Panamanian economy. At the same time, some of that is bound to happen.' Apart from the hard-line Elliott Abrams at the State Department, hardly anyone in the US government liked sanctions: their use was due in large measure to the overwhelming pressure coming from Congress to 'do something'. The House of

Representatives approved a resolution on the subject by 367 votes to only two against.

Those who argued that they would not work were proved correct. Noriega survived the March onslaught, and later attempts to refine the sanctions weapon by singling out businesses linked to the regime were equally futile. But Washington refused to give up, right to the last, pre-invasion minute. On 30 November 1989 it announced a ban on Panamanian-registered ships using US ports as from 1 February 1990, a move greeted with outrage in the shipping community, and subsequently rendered irrelevant by the invasion.

By this stage the opposition within Panama felt thoroughly disillusioned with the sanctions policy. Ricardo Arias Calderón said of the shipping ban that it would 'only make the crisis worse and increase poverty.' In a statement on 29 November 1989, Endara, Arias Calderón and Ford criticised US policy, saying 'we disagree with general sanctions that affect the Panamanian people, whose human and economic sacrifices to achieve democracy have been and continue to be exemplary.' Sanctions were hurting the Civic Crusade's members, who demanded instead a rapid escalation of pressure. So worried were they by the effects that they called off a highly effective strike 'in view of the new financial situation which is aggravating still further the lamentable state of the Panamanian economy.'

The private sector, the Church, and virtually every opposition party complained about the policy in late April 1988, and their protests were supported even by Delvalle.

One US official commented drily that the sanctions had 'ruined a healthy capitalist economy, weakened a pro-American middle class and created the conditions for the growth of communist influence in Panama. You have to admit that's quite a diplomatic achievement.'

In fact, the Panamanian economy had been in serious trouble well before the sanctions campaign began. The international banking centre, once the biggest in Latin America, had begun to decline as the debt crisis struck the region in the early 1980s. This coincided with a period of bank deregulation in the US which reduced the value of offshore banking centres such as Panama. By the end of 1986 Panama itself had — according to the World Bank — the biggest per capita debt outside the industrialised world: $4.8 billion for a population of only 2.3 million people. The budgeted fiscal deficit — the gap between the government's income and expenditure — hit $140 million for 1987, and this figure more than doubled as the Civic Crusade's non-payment campaign, coupled with economic slump, began to hit tax revenues.

The Panamanian economy depended heavily on service activities like banking, shipping and insurance. Political stability was essential

Figleaf currency. Although named the *Balboa*, the Panamanian currency is interchangeable with the US dollar.   (Carlos Reyes, ANDES Press Agency)

to its well-being, and unlike manufacturing industry, businesses like banks could move their assets out overnight if they smelled trouble. Capital flight to more secure locations, like the Bahamas and the Cayman Islands, began as soon as the first demonstrators hit the streets in June 1987. By the end of the year deposits in the banking centre had fallen to about $23 billion, from $32 billion a year earlier. The domestic banking system too suffered from capital flight.

As the crisis began to bite, Panama suspended repayments on its foreign debt, and by October 1989 arrears amounted to $1.2 billion. The country's gross domestic product (GDP — the value of all the goods and services produced in the economy) fell by over 17 per cent in 1988. In late 1989, not long before the invasion, the government had to introduce what it called 'war measures', including a wage freeze and changes in price and tax regulations. Some sources put unemployment as high as 45 per cent.

Despite such economic collapse, Noriega survived. Roberto Brenes, an opposition businessman and newspaper owner, pointed out that 'when you earn your cash from money laundering, drug trafficking and arms dealing for the Iran-Iraq war, you aren't as vulnerable personally to sanctions. The money he hands out to his soldiers doesn't depend much on economic activity.'

However, there was more to it than the FDP's sources of illicit money. In the first place, numerous exemptions weakened the sanctions. The company running the trans-isthmian oil pipeline was allowed to pay its taxes, for fear that the oil would be stopped; the US embassy had to pay its electricity and phone bills in case it was cut off, and so on. Many private businesses also evaded the restrictions.

There were also thousands of Panamanian employees of the US military and the Canal Commission, who continued to receive their wages, which fed into the rest of the economy. The Colón Free Zone continued to function normally, as did most of Panamanian agriculture. With a history of clandestine business activities behind him (including helping Cuba to evade US sanctions), Noriega was not about to go under without exploiting every available loophole.

The government began to pay its employees with negotiable cheques, which to some extent replaced cash, while the Banking Commission authorised the use of certificates (CEDIs) for those with savings accounts who wished to purchase major items, such as vehicles.

The crisis forced the private sector to find its own ways round the sanctions. The president of the Panamanian Union of Industrialists (SIP) reported that 'in the industrial sector, as in the óthers, [we] have been creative in finding solutions to the problems and have found ways of paying our workers with vouchers, formulae for solving the problems of clients who had no way of paying, and all kinds of methods of solving financial problems.'

Latin American nations as ideologically diverse as Cuba and Chile condemned sanctions as 'coercive' and refused to help close any loopholes. The rest of the world declined to follow the US lead, leaving the Panamanian regime battered but still in place. Indeed, Noriega played on the sanctions campaign as yet more proof of his status as a lone fighter against the evil empire.

The Reagan administration hoped that US economic and political pressure would provoke such unrest and generate such substantial costs that the leadership of the Defence Forces would be induced to break with Noriega and send him packing. But Washington overlooked the possibility that the leadership of the FDP might regard its authority and ability to rule as being seriously undermined by a capitulation to the US. Whether Noriega was liked or disliked by his fellow officers, to remove him in response to US pressure would be to raise doubts that the Panamanian military had the power and resolve to govern.

Election Countdown

Few observers of the Panamanian scene in mid-1988 gave much for Noriega's chances of surviving to supervise the general election for 1989. In addition to the damage caused by US economic sanctions and political instability, Washington was working overtime on other schemes to bring the general down or negotiate him out of power. 'Every effort we can take to foster discontent . . . I can assure you we are taking,' said one senior US official.

Washington came up with at least five notionally 'covert' plans, including one which involved setting up Delvalle's provisional government on a US base. The Pentagon ruled out the scheme but not before it had cost Colonel Eduardo Herrera Hassán his job. Herrera was a Noriega opponent who had been packed off to serve as Panamanian ambassador to Israel. Recruited secretly by the State Department to serve as Delvalle's military chief, and encourage FDP defections, he was sacked by Noriega two weeks after the plan was vetoed. Thereafter he began working with the CIA on plans for the general's overthrow.

In mid-May Noriega agreed to a deal (negotiated by State Department envoy Michael Kozak) that would have meant his stepping down in August and leaving the country in exchange for the dropping of the Florida indictments. This was the closest Washington came to a negotiated departure, and despite the unpopularity of 'doing a deal with a drug trafficker' the administration seemed prepared to go ahead with it.

In the end the agreement was never concluded, primarily because of a sequence of contradictory statements and sudden ultimatums by the White House and State Department. Other concerns intervened, such as a US-Soviet presidential summit, and with a US election coming up in November it proved impossible to revive the negotiations, even though Noriega stated, both in public and private, that 'we are ready to talk with all those who do not come to us with ultimatums.'

Disagreements in Washington between the different branches of the government, and even between President Reagan and Vice-President George Bush, largely explain the failure to get rid of Noriega by peaceful means. The general's own public statement at the time accurately assessed what had happened.

'On several occasions, Panama accepted changes proposed by advisers of the Vice-President in order to protect his presidential campaign. However, even that was not enough. The US wanted an immediate agreement.'

With the US election approaching, Bush let it be known that, for the first time in eight years, he disagreed with President Reagan on a major policy issue. As the Republican candidate in November, former CIA director Bush could not afford to be associated with a deal struck with Noriega, whose past links with the agency became a campaign issue. In May 1988 Bush was trailing Democratic contender Michael Dukakis by ten points in the opinion polls.

Military action was equally out of the question at a time when failure could mean electoral defeat. The only alternative was to try to keep Panama out of the headlines and downplay any talk of a deal. Pressure from the Bush camp was probably the single most important factor in derailing the talks on Noriega's departure, which in turn made military intervention that much more likely.

A further plan involved military action by exiled FDP personnel headed by Colonel Herrera, but the Senate Select Committee on Intelligence saw it as ill-considered and refused to give the go-ahead. The committee allegedly feared that the plan might end with the death of Noriega, thereby violating the Executive Order which forbade US involvement in assassinations of foreign leaders. When Herrera's 'National Concord Movement' did distribute leaflets calling for a military uprising, it merely triggered an FDP crack-down leading to 26 arrests.

The Reagan-Bush transition period brought no fresh initiatives, except a (rejected) offer by Delvalle to negotiate with Noriega. By December 1988 the opposition had little alternative but to participate in the 1989 election in the hope of winning a 'Panamanian victory'. As one opposition activist put it, 'whether we run or not, Noriega is going to steal the elections anyway, but if we refuse to participate, we will be allowing him to claim that his victory was legitimate.' The decision to contest the election came on 3 January 1989, under strong encouragement from the US embassy.

Up to the last minute, Noriega kept open the option of standing for the presidency himself, although in order to do so he would have had to resign as head of the FDP. He even pushed through a legal amendment reducing from six months to three the period required between his retirement and candidacy. In the end, however, the official National Liberation Coalition (COLINA — the new name for the ruling UNADE alliance) backed the candidacy of Noriega crony Carlos Duque. Duque was a PRD leader and long-standing business partner of Noriega who ran a company called Transit SA, part of the network used to circumvent the US embargo on Cuba and a major source of 'back-door' funds for the FDP.

The Democratic Opposition Alliance (ADO, renamed ADOC with the addition of the Civic Crusade) immediately ran into difficulties. Arnulfo Arias, the veteran populist who could have attracted the working class vote, had died the previous August and the Alliance's member parties could not agree on a presidential candidate. Moreover, Arias's Authentic *Panameñista* Party (PPA) split and the faction that backed the government won legal control of the party.

The major contenders for the opposition candidacy were Ricardo Arias Calderón of the Christian Democrats (PDC) and Guillermo Endara of the PPA. Fierce internal battles over the issue ended with Endara heading the ticket and Arias being nominated as candidate for the first vice presidency. Guillermo (Billy) Ford became the second vice-presidential candidate.

The election took place on 7 May in the presence of an estimated 400 foreign observers, including former US President Jimmy Carter. Exit polls conducted by the Carter team and the Catholic Church suggested a massive 3:1 victory for ADOC, much bigger than the official fraud machine could manage.

Noriega had taken the usual precautions, including manipulating the voter registration lists to make it harder for opposition supporters to vote; giving FDP personnel freedom to vote at any polling station they chose (thus allowing them to vote repeatedly); and ensuring there were enough parties in the offical coalition to out-vote ADOC in any dispute within the electoral tribunal. When it became clear that this was not enough, the FDP resorted to militarising the polling stations, forging the vote tallies and eventually suspending the count.

A furious Carter called an impromptu press conference to announce that the regime was 'taking the elections by fraud'. But both government and opposition seemed stunned by the scale of Noriega's electoral defeat. Not until the Wednesday following the Sunday election did the ADOC leaders — once more urged on by the US embassy — stage a demonstration to demand that their victory be recognised. The response came in the form of an attack by the paramilitary Dignity Battalions.

According to Amnesty International:

> 'official forces were said to have used guns, water cannons, lead pipes, baseball bats, clubs and stones to attack unarmed opposition leaders and supporters carrying out demonstrations to protest at what they described as irregularities during the elections and falsification of their results.'

All three ADOC leaders suffered injuries; three people died and over 300 were arrested in the aftermath of the election. One of the dead was Alexis Guerra, Ford's bodyguard, who was shot at point-blank range. Pictures of Ford himself, his shirt covered with Guerra's blood, being beaten by one of Noriega's thugs, were shown around the world. This single image seemed to sum up the regime's brutality; it would later be invoked by George Bush in his justifications of the invasion.

Within Panama, however, it had the required effect of terrorising the opposition. A general strike, called for the week after the demonstration, fizzled out, and although ADOC leaders' denied that they were holding out for a US intervention, that seemed to be precisely what many of their followers wanted. 'At the US embassy telephones ring persistently with callers requesting an invasion,' one journalist wrote.

As if to encourage these hopes, President Bush sent in an extra 2,000 troops, whose arrival merely served to buttress Noriega's excuse for annulling the election — that foreign interference had prevented a fair poll. A clumsy US attempt to influence the result with a $10 million plan for covert support to the opposition also handed the general a propaganda coup.

Washington seemed as uncertain over what to do next as the Panamanian opposition. 'The ball is in his [Noriega's] court,' said White House press secretary Marlin Fitzwater. An invasion remained on the table, but the cautious Bush was still not ready. As Senator Richard Lugar put it, 'the next step is consultation with every other country that has interests, and many certainly do.'

Latin America Steps In

A good deal of opprobrium has been heaped on the Organization of American States, both in Washington and by the Panamanian opposition, for its alleged unwillingness to confront Noriega and force him from office. When Panama's neighbours in Latin America criticised the invasion and its aftermath, they were met by scornful

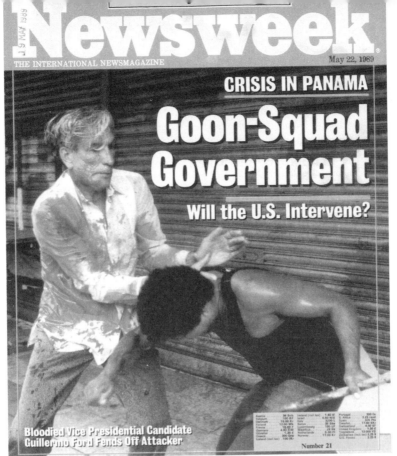

Newsweek

THE INTERNATIONAL NEWSMAGAZINE

May 22, 1989

19 MAY 1989

CRISIS IN PANAMA

Goon-Squad Government

Will the U.S. Intervene?

Bloodied Vice Presidential Candidate
Guillermo Ford Fends Off Attacker

Number 21

Pictures of vice-presidential candidate Guillermo Ford, covered with the blood
of his murdered bodyguard and under attack from Noriega's thugs, shocked
the world.

reminders that Latin American nations had failed to achieve the
regional solution most of them saw as the best alternative.

The first response by the OAS to the Panamanian crisis came on 1
July 1987, when it approved a resolution calling on the US to stop
interfering in Panama's internal affairs. There were 17 votes in favour,
one against and eight abstentions (four countries were not
represented). At the end of March 1988 an Extraordinary Congress of
the Latin American Economic System (SELA) called for the lifting of
US economic sanctions, which it described as 'coercive'. Its resolution
also raised the possibility of economic aid to Panama. All Latin
American states, including Cuba, belong to SELA, but the US is not a
member.

The original proposal for the Congress referred to the sanctions as 'economic aggression', and most neighbouring countries certainly saw them as such. The president of Costa Rica, Nobel prize-winner Oscar Arias, said sanctions only hurt the people of Panama and would not resolve the problem.

A senior Latin American diplomat in Washington said, 'we are not so naive as to think Noriega is wonderful. On the other hand, American intervention is bad, a violation of our basic principles. It has become very worrisome for many.' Sol Linowitz, President Carter's special ambassador for the canal treaty negotiations in 1977, said of the Latin American nations, 'what troubles them is that in their eyes this is economic intervention. And when they look upon what is going on in Panama, they see this as a precedent that could be used in their country if in the judgment of the US it becomes necessary.'

The SELA meeting came after the collapse of the Delvalle government, but even before that moves were afoot which could perhaps have provided an alternative to the US 'big stick'. Three former Latin American presidents — Alfonso López Michelsen of Colombia, Carlos Andrés Pérez of Venezuela and Daniel Oduber of Costa Rica — had met the main protagonists in Panama the week before Delvalle's absurd 'dismissal' of Noriega. The three presidents came very close to reaching an agreement, drawing up a plan which would have gone into effect on 7 March, ten days after Delvalle made his move. The plan envisaged an interim government, headed by Delvalle, and clean elections in 1989, followed by the appointment of a new general staff of the FDP, subject to civilian control.

The plan failed when Delvalle, who was a party to the agreement, went ahead with his move against Noriega and Washington gave the green light for the March coup attempt. Pérez subsequently described Delvalle's action as 'unfortunate and unnecessary', adding that the alternative had been virtually in place. It is hard to avoid the conclusion that Washington deliberately sabotaged the Latin American plan.

This would have been perfectly consistent with the US attitude to regional peace plans in general. The previous August, when Central American presidents were on the point of agreeing to the Arias Plan (or Esquipulas II), aimed at resolving armed conflict in the region, the Reagan White House had suddenly presented its own alternative proposals. Those present at the Guatemala City meeting had no doubt that the move was a deliberate attempt to head off a non-US solution, although in the event it seems to have caused such resentment that the Arias Plan went through anyway.

Throughout the period in which the Contadora Group was seeking a solution to the Central American crisis, the US exerted pressure on its members (Mexico, Panama, Venezuela and Colombia) aimed at bringing them into line with Washington's policy. It could be argued that sanctions against Noriega began in January 1986, when Washington transferred a $40 million economic package from Panama to Guatemala, allegedly to punish Noriega for not giving adequate support to the US campaign against Nicaragua.

On 16 April 1988, Oscar Arias himself proposed bringing forward the Panama election (scheduled for May 1989) as part of a solution to the crisis, but this and other Latin American suggestions failed to take off. Not until the May 1989 fiasco was over did regional efforts once again become important.

The Group of Eight Latin American nations (from whose membership Panama had been suspended) expressed its 'deep concern' on 10 May, saying Panama was in danger of distancing itself still further from its neighbours. On the following day, George Bush called for a joint Latin American effort to remove Noriega. Venezuela and Peru had begun to take the lead in seeking a regional solution, and the OAS accepted a Venezuelan proposal for a meeting to discuss the 'serious crisis' in Panama. This took place on 18-19 May 1989.

However, the OAS was an organisation in decline. Set up in 1948 at a meeting in Bogotá, Colombia, it served in its early history as a regional rubber-stamp for US interventionism. Among nationalists it became known as the US 'ministry for the colonies', not least because it had its headquarters in Washington. Perhaps its most ignoble moments were the 1962 decision to expel Cuba and its 1965 provision of a diplomatic and military figleaf for the US invasion of the Dominican Republic.

As unwavering support for US foreign policy became less fashionable, Washington grew tired of the OAS. By May 1989, the US had fallen $51 million in arrears on its annual payments (the lion's share of the OAS budget), and the organisation could barely pay its 600 staff (despite the recent dismissal of another 300). The decision to hold the emergency meetings on Panama strained its resources to the limit.

Virtually every country in the region — with the exception of Nicaragua and Cuba — condemned the Noriega regime for its conduct of the election. Even the Mexican government, normally the least inclined to promote interventionism, declared Noriega 'morally and ethically' unfit to lead Panama. The US lobbied hard to have the general's name included in the final resolution, which in the event proved much harsher than most observers had expected.

By 20 votes to two, with seven abstentions, the OAS declared that the Noriega regime's actions had 'limited the right of the Panamanian people to freely elect their legitimate authorities' and that the worsening crisis 'could give rise to serious threats to international peace and security'. It blamed the general personally for 'outrageous abuses perpetrated against the opposition candidates and citizenry,' and authorised OAS secretary general João Baena Soares and three foreign ministers from the region to visit Panama and seek a formula for a 'transfer of power in the shortest possible time and with full respect for the sovereign will of the Panamanian people.' However the OAS statement also called for the full respect of the sovereignty of Panama and full compliance with the Panama Canal Treaties.

The foreign ministers came from Ecuador, Guatemala and Trinidad & Tobago. By far the most experienced among them was Diego Cordovez of Ecuador, the architect of the UN plan for the Soviet withdrawal from Afghanistan. The delegation arrived in Panama City four days later, to be met by statements from the ruling PRD and the government-controlled press saying that they had no moral or legal authority to interfere in Panamanian affairs. This was especially disconcerting, since Panama's own foreign minister, Jorge Ritter, was a party to the agreement, and the government had initially welcomed the move.

Altogether, the OAS delegation visited Panama on four occasions between late May and mid-August. Their efforts were hindered when the regime declared that Noriega's position was non-negotiable, while the opposition would not contemplate any deal which left him in place or failed to recognise its victory in the May election.

The atmosphere did not improve when Washington insisted on an instant solution. The US reinforced the point with deliberately provocative military manoeuvres and barely-veiled threats to take military action if a multilateral solution could not be found. After reinforcing its Southcom garrison by an extra 2,000 troops, the US sent armed military convoys across Panamanian territory with orders not to be deterred by roadblocks or FDP personnel. 'We're obviously doing it only to make a point,' one official told a foreign journalist. Clashes between US and Panamanian military units multiplied, and in one incident a US soldier was accidentally shot by his own side. When the OAS delegation produced its final report, it criticised the 'negative effect' of these manoeuvres on the negotiations.

The unreasonable time limit imposed by the US delegation was equally negative. When the first report on negotiations indicated that the parties had reached 'a measure of agreement', the US argued for an extension of only two more weeks to reach a settlement. Eventually,

Washington accepted a compromise of six weeks, but again, the words and actions of the US delegation suggested that Washington would accept a multilateral solution only if it produced precisely the required result in the shortest possible time. More cynical observers concluded that the US had raised such a possibility only in order to discount it, thus paving the way for unilateral action.

In all, the OAS spent three months in its attempt to negotiate a solution; a ridiculously short time when set against any comparable situation. The end came when the term of office of stand-in president Manuel Solís Palma expired on 31 August and the regime found another obliging nonentity — Comptroller General Francisco Rodríguez — to inaugurate as provisional president. At this point Erick Arturo Delvalle's dubious claim to the presidency vanished altogether, rendering him obsolete even from Washington's point of view.

The OAS acknowledged that, 'the continued presence of General Noriega as commander-in-chief of the Defence Forces has been identified both by supporters and opposition as one of the factors, if not the principal factor, which must be addressed in order to solve the crisis.' His departure was one of the elements regarded as crucial, along with the formation of a transition government, fresh elections and the lifting of the measures imposed by the US.

US Acting Secretary of State Lawrence Eagleburger, addressing the last OAS meeting before 31 August, in effect declared the effort dead when he announced that, 'if the terms of the OAS mandate have not been met by 1 September, then the Noriega regime will have declared itself to be an outlaw among civilised nations and we should treat it accordingly.'

Most of the diplomatic corps boycotted Rodríguez' inauguration and Latin American governments began withdrawing their ambassadors. However, they still resisted Washington's call for region-wide sanctions to match its own. Their negotiators had identified these as part of the problem, rather than the solution.

The evidence suggests that even after 1 September a negotiated settlement could still have headed off the invasion. The Panamanian government stated that fresh elections would follow once 'US interference' ended. This would also have been acceptable to the opposition, despite its earlier insistence on recognition of its May election victory. In October 1989, after the second coup attempt had failed, Spanish Prime Minister Felipe González proposed fresh elections, which he believed had the approval of the ADOC leaders.

By this time, however, Washington had opted for the military solution, and no amount of talking would have made any difference.

Perhaps the Latin American response to the annulment of the May election results should have been stronger, but it is unlikely that this would have deflected Washington from its course. The responsibility for the weakness of regional institutions in large measure lies with successive US governments. If the Bush administration genuinely wanted a regional settlement, it set about getting one in a very curious way.

As Larry Birns of the Council on Hemispheric Affairs noted, after the failure of the OAS effort:

> 'It was sheer hypocrisy for [the US] to stand before the OAS and strongly call upon it to take the decisive action against Noriega that Washington had refused to do for most of the 1980s.'

A Failed Coup

> '[The US government] is like a dog that barks and barks but never bites.' (Ricardo Arias Calderón, after the October coup)

By October 1989, the prospects for a peaceful resolution of Washington's Panama problem looked increasingly remote. There remained a few more weapons in the US economic arsenal (such as the shipping ban, announced in November), but it was apparent that the Panamanian economy, though badly damaged, was not about to collapse altogether. Having effectively scuppered both bilateral and multilateral negotiations, the US had two realistic options: it could do nothing, or it could use force.

Inaction meant leaving Noriega in place and admitting defeat on an issue which Reagan and Bush had raised to the status of a moral crusade. However, a military solution might yet be possible without the use of US troops, if only Washington would induce the FDP to take matters into its own hands. Unfortunately for Washington, US links to FDP officers were by now minimal.

After the rather feeble coup attempt of March 1988 Noriega had reorganised his officer corps, placing proven loyalists in all the most sensitive positions and discouraging further mutinies by parading the beaten and humiliated rebels before FDP personnel all over the country. Noriega promoted to major Captain Moisés Giroldi, who had played a prominent role in putting down the 1988 attempt, and put him in charge of security at the *Comandancia*.

Seemingly above suspicion, and with constant access to the general, Giroldi was the perfect man to head a successful bid to oust Noriega.

He had become convinced that such a step was necessary for the FDP's survival, and had won over not only the head of special forces, Captain Jesús Balma, but also Major Federico Olechea, the commander of Battalion 2000. Noriega relied on this elite unit, formed to defend the canal after its handover at the end of the century, and its support — or at least its neutrality — was vital.

But Giroldi also needed the assistance of the US military in blocking off access roads to the *Comandancia* while the coup was under way. This would ensure that any loyal troops — especially the so-called *Machos de Monte*, the Cuban-trained 7th Rifle Company, based at Rio Hato to the west of the capital — could not come to the general's aid.

He made contact with the CIA which seems to have convinced him that US assistance would be given. But as the coup attempt began it became apparent that the support was hesitant and patchy. Although they blocked some roads, US forces left open the highway to the east and allowed the *Machos de Monte* to fly into the military side of Tocumen airport. Accompanied by Battalion 2000, whose commander decided to keep his options open, they moved to surround the *Comandancia*, where Giroldi held Noriega at gunpoint.

Besieged, and barely able to communicate with US officials, Giroldi eventually surrendered. According to some sources he offered to hand over Noriega to the US — an offer which Washington turned down. Noriega's troops later tortured and killed Giroldi and at least ten of the coup leaders.

In the US, President Bush faced angry criticism of his unwillingness to commit US forces in aid of Giroldi. Hardly any politicians or commentators wondered if this might not be an internal Panamanian matter in which the US had no business interfering. Administration officials claimed that Bush had felt constrained by congressionally-imposed restrictions on US involvement in any coup which might lead to the death of the leader concerned. Whatever the truth of this, Washington did not want to see a *torrijista* like Giroldi take over, and his offer to hand over Noriega was unwelcome at a time when the administration still thought it could avoid the embarrassment of a trial.

In any event, the failed coup brought about a situation in which a US invasion became almost inevitable. Now the potential FDP dissidents had revealed themselves a fresh coup attempt would be out of the question for some time, especially after military colleagues had seen the fate of Giroldi and his men. Public opinion in the US attacked the 'wimpish' behaviour of the president. And many Panamanians were more than ever convinced that only Washington could provide the solution.

The coup plotters seem never to have considered the possibility of involving the civilian opposition in their plans; while the leadership of the latter confined itself to criticising the US for not acting. As one anonymous ADOC dissident put it, 'what is the opposition doing? It requires risks to get rid of Noriega, but they are not prepared to take them.' A civilian uprising in support of the coup, the dissident argued, might have allowed it to succeed, providing a last-minute Panamanian solution. As it was, the time for such a solution was now past, and although the Panamanians did not know it, the countdown to the 20 December invasion had begun.

Chapter 5
Picking up the Pieces

Once the dust of the invasion had settled, the Endara government's first task was to establish its legitimacy. Although Endara himself had won a convincing victory in the May 1989 election, Panamanians had voted as a protest against the Noriega regime, rather than to endorse Endara or his policies. Further, Endara's government in 1990 bore little resemblance to that promised in May 1989: the country remained under US occupation, with US civilian and military personnel taking the important decisions. Doubts over the new government's legitimacy also sprang from the manner of its investiture, sworn in on a US military base just hours before the invasion, and its reluctance to call fresh elections to confirm its mandate to govern.

The invasion itself had proved overwhelmingly popular, even allowing for the doubtful accuracy of opinion polls carried out under a state of military occupation. However, its popularity stemmed from anti-Noriega feeling and the population's desire for a rapid recovery of the economy, reduced to chaos by a combination of US economic sanctions, structural defects and the destruction and looting accompanying the invasion. Recovery depended on Washington sending immediate and substantial economic aid.

The speed and the manner in which the Endara team came to power left its members somewhat dazed. In January 1990 the head of public relations in Ford's Planning Ministry revealed that the government had handed over to the Chamber of Commerce the whole task of calculating the invasion damage, failing to grasp that damaged government buildings were its own responsibility. 'They still think they're the private sector,' she said.

The Pentagon's destruction of the FDP left the new regime needing to create some kind of security forces out of the wreckage. That in turn meant deciding whether this should include an army, and where to obtain the new recruits. However, the new government was by no means united, once the common enemy who had held the coalition together had left the scene.

There were three main forces in the ADOC government: Endara's own *Arnulfistas*, the inheritors of the tradition of Arnulfo Arias, whose lack of a party had forced them to stand in the election under the banner of the Authentic Liberal Party (PLA); Ford's MOLIRENA party, another Liberal tendency, made up primarily of bankers and industrialists; and the Christian Democrats (PDC) of Ricardo Arias Calderón.

Endara soon formed an *Arnulfista* Party, and in May it acquired legal status, backed by the signatures of 115,000 supporters. The new party demanded a reallocation of cabinet seats, most of which had gone to the PDC, provoking disagreement with the Christian Democrats. As early as 18 January Endara supporters staged a demonstration against the PDC's 'monopoly' on government posts.

Although Ford's party had no mass base, he controlled not only the finance and planning ministries but also foreign affairs (through Julio Linares). This gave him power over the negotiation and distribution of all international reconstruction aid. However the position carried certain disadvantages: if the economy failed to recover, or if corruption became apparent, the blame would be laid at Ford's door.

The PDC was the most powerful element in the coalition, despite Arias Calderón's reputation as a humourless and uncharismatic leader. The PDC leader had sought the presidency for most of the past decade, but each time there was an election he found himself playing second (or even third) fiddle to the *Arnulfistas*. The PDC had grown into an important opposition force during the latter half of the 1980s, largely as a result of its consistent stand against military rule and its alliances with older, richer parties. When the new government reconstructed the results of the 1989 election, the PDC won almost half the seats in the legislature, and was undoubtedly the party with the greatest number of members prepared for government.

Arias Calderón held the interior and justice portfolios, which gave him control over the formation of the new Public Force (FP), created to replace the FDP. If handled correctly, these posts could make him Panama's effective ruler in coming decades. The PDC also held the welfare ministries of health, education, housing and public works, along with many local government posts, all of which could extend its base beyond the lawyers, teachers, students and businessmen who made up most of its members. Internationally, it enjoyed the backing of the Christian Democrat International, of which Arias Calderón himself was vice-president.

President Guillermo Endara surrounded by US bodyguards, visits a makeshift refugee camp for those made homeless by the US invasion, Christmas Day 1989

International Isolation

Although Panama's new, post-invasion government was initially popular inside the country, much of Latin America as a whole saw Endara as a mere puppet of the US. The chorus of criticism even led some US officials to call on Endara to hold fresh elections, or at least a plebiscite, in order to legitimise his administration. Endara's team indignantly declined, describing such advice as (in the words of foreign minister Julio Linares) 'an act of intervention'. The irony of the phrase, it seems, escaped them.

Regional bodies were unanimous in their condemnation of the invasion and their calls for fresh elections. The Organization of American States approved a resolution 'deeply deploring' the US military intervention, with only the US itself voting against. The Latin American Parliament 'energetically condemned' the invasion. Most Latin American countries declined to recognise the Endara government, with Peruvian President Alan García calling it 'not legitimate' and a country 'governed by the State Department, the Pentagon, Southcom and the US troops.' In retaliation, the new government expelled Peru's chargé d'affaires.

The US forces had antagonised Latin American governments during the invasion by repeatedly violating diplomatic immunity. In addition to the siege of the Vatican's Nunciature, where Noriega had sought refuge (see Appendix 1), troops surrounded other embassies where leading members of his ousted regime were sheltered. The Cuban ambassador was detained for an hour and a half by US troops, and in the worst incident of all the Nicaraguan ambassador's residence was raided, despite its diplomatic status. The US was compelled to use its veto to prevent the United Nations Security Council approving a resolution denouncing the raid. Washington claimed its apology for the incident was enough.

In early January President Bush announced that Vice-President Dan Quayle would tour Latin America to show that the US sought to be a 'friendly, supportive and respectful neighbour'. Despite protests from several Latin American governments, Quayle's tour went ahead, but the only Latin American countries that would receive him were Panama and Honduras, another country highly dependent on US patronage.

At the end of March 1990, Panama was finally expelled from the Group of Eight Latin American nations (it had been suspended after Noriega removed Delvalle from the presidency). Endara particularly blamed the Mexicans, whom he considered to be behind the resolution, and accused the Mexican foreign minister of belonging to a 'corrupt party' which held power by electoral fraud. Gradually, however, the diplomatic problems eased, and most countries quietly returned their ambassadors to Panama City, although the international standing of the Endara government remained low.

The Opposition

The almost total lack of coherent opposition gave the new government a significant advantage. In an opinion poll commissioned by CBS News in late January, 92 per cent of respondents said they supported the invasion. The FDP had been destroyed, and its civilian allies of the Democratic Revolutionary Party (PRD) were in disarray, with many of them either in hiding or under arrest. When the National Assembly reconvened, it awarded the PRD only six out of 67 parliamentary seats.

The trade union and popular movement too, large parts of which had been compromised by their association with the military regime, struggled to find an independent voice.

An armed opposition group calling itself the 20 December Movement (M-20) quickly appeared on the scene, with a grenade

Short-lived euphoria greeted the fall of Noriega   (Bill Robinson/*The Observer*)

attack on a bar in which one US serviceman was killed. In its communiqués, M-20 described itself as a 'nationalist and revolutionary' group, and denied supporting Noriega. But its operations were sporadic and largely ineffectual: they did not suggest the existence of a true guerrilla nucleus, and there was no indication of popular support.

If the Endara team hoped for a honeymoon, however, it was soon disappointed. Even the opinion poll results were not necessarily trustworthy: as one Panamanian, a veteran of the Sandinista guerrilla campaign in Nicaragua, told the *Washington Post*, 'there aren't any civil rights. Who's going to tell an army of occupation they don't like Endara? It's asking for big trouble.'

Yet many Panamanians welcomed the invasion. According to Chuchu Martínez, a noted Panamanian poet and friend of the late Omar Torrijos, it was largely through opposition to Noriega, rather than support for his opponents.

> 'We Panamanians have been suffering a hell of an economic crisis for years and the Noriega government in recent years has not been noted for passing popular measures. On the contrary, the war laws went against the interests of the people. The only

progressive thing was the confrontation with the imperialists but there was no national project, not even the intention of satisfying the needs of the people.'

There was no shortage of post-invasion grievances. Many of the refugees and the relatives of those who had died blamed the new government rather than the US for their plight. Washington eventually provided about 3,000 of the refugees with makeshift accommodation in an aircraft hangar at the Albrook air base, while 500 or so more remained in two schools. At least another 10,000 had to fend for themselves. The US paid an average of $6,500 to families who had lost everything in the invasion.

The unemployed, and especially the 15,000 public employees who lost their jobs in the first six months of the post-invasion government, formed another potentially restive group. On 20 June the El Chorrillo Committee of War Refugees, the Association of Relatives of Victims of the Invasion and the National Federation of Public Servants and Employees — together with other trade union and student bodies — staged a well-attended march to mark the sixth month of the US military intervention and demand action on the refugee issue. Despite government concessions, the refugees made it clear they would consider 'other forms of protest' if the authorities did not provide rapid solutions to their plight.

The trade union movement attempted to reorganise itself. 'We'll have to keep our heads down for the first few months,' said one leading member of the Authentic Workers' Central (CAT), 'but if the government does not satisfy the demands of the population in terms of work and housing, this situation could explode in a couple of months.'

The government and the private sector made it clear from the outset that they wanted changes to the Labour Code 'in order to assist the economic recovery'. According to Alfredo Maduro of the Chamber of Commerce, 'the good worker doesn't need laws to assist him.' Against the background of unemployment estimated at 35 per cent, the labour movement could scarcely allow such a view to go unchallenged.

The most important labour organisation under the military regime, CONATO, had little credibility left. After initially suggesting that it would create a 'third force' between government and opposition for the May 1989 election, CONATO eventually opted to back the official COLINA alliance, and now the need for an independent and unified workers' organisation was more urgent than ever.

In November 1989, a part of the labour movement headed by the Confederation of Workers of the Republic of Panama (CTRP) had

A week after the invasion, Panamanians who lost their homes in the invasion await processing for entry into a refugee camp. (Bill Robinson/*The Observer*)

attempted to create a unified trade union body. Their intention was to strengthen CONATO or create a new organisation, but their efforts had been interrupted by the invasion. Unions which had opposed the military regime came together after the invasion to form the General Union of Workers (UGT), with the aim of purging the labour movement of those leaders who had compromised themselves by associating with the FDP. However, the task of constructing a genuinely independent trade union body representing all workers would take time. More than two decades of reliance on military populism would not be easy to wipe away.

Even the Catholic Church, whose Archbishop Marcos McGrath had initially welcomed the invasion as 'an act of liberation', in August issued a pastoral letter criticising the Panamanian and US governments. The letter referred to 'the appearance of the old vices of the struggle for political space' within the government, adding that 'each party in the alliance seems to think it has the right to demand its share of power and economic benefits.' Unemployment, sackings, the slow administration of justice and the interference of the US in internal Panamanian affairs had characterised the first seven months after the invasion, the bishops concluded.

Back in Charge

By the end of February 1990, the US government completed its troop withdrawal, as demanded by Panama's Latin American neighbours as a condition for recognising the Endara government. In practice this meant reducing troop levels to the same level as immediately prior to the invasion (about 13,600, including the extra 2,000 Bush had ordered in after the May election). As even Foreign Minister Linares recognised, 'Panama is a country occupied by the US army.'

This did not mean that US forces were complying with the requirements of the 1977 treaties. US forces had occupied a number of the so-called 'reverted areas', which the treaties had returned to Panama. These included several bases and three strategic islands at the entrance to the canal. Only when a US Army official made the mistake of declaring that the Panamanians had 'temporarily ceded' control of the islands did the Endara government demand their return.

However, with no credible security forces of its own, the new government found it hard to object to US military patrols throughout Panamanian territory. US military police with automatic weapons patrolled urban areas jointly with unarmed or lightly armed FP personnel; while in places as distant as Darién province, on the Colombian border, peasants reported being stopped at gunpoint by US special forces and asked for identification. The official US version described the green berets as on 'routine training exercises'.

The Panamanian government, pressed to explain the situation, replied that 'because of the special circumstances' US troops had been given permission to patrol rural areas, but that such patrols would not continue indefinitely. The troops themselves were under instructions to hunt down guerrillas and drug traffickers. 'Submissiveness to the US government,' noted the newspaper *La Estrella de Panamá*, 'seems to be the current historical pattern.'

Immediately after the invasion, US embassy officials or Southcom took every important decision. 'President Endara did not know he had imposed a curfew until the US military told him so,' one journalist wrote. Southcom adopted the habit of making announcements in the name of the Panamanian government. US troops took on a policing role, arresting civilians for questioning on non-military matters. Deane Hinton, veteran of El Salvador and other sticky situations, soon replaced Ambassador Arthur Davis, a political appointee well out of his depth. Meanwhile, Davis' deputy, John Bushnell, moved into a spacious suite next to President Endara in the foreign ministry (the government's temporary home). Vice-Presidents Arias and Ford made do with more humble accommodation on the floor below. Little effort was made to conceal the reality of the relationship. One US official put it bluntly: 'the embassy is in operational control.'

Assistant Secretary of State Lawrence Eagleburger put it slightly differently when he addressed a press conference at the embassy in early January. 'The US government,' he said, 'plans to be actively engaged with the new Panamanian leadership as they shift their economy towards development of the private sector and expansion of economic opportunities for all Panamanians.'

The Mexican newspaper *Excelsior* explored the precise meaning of 'actively engaged' a couple of months later. It described a complete 'parallel government', composed of 31 US officials, both civilian and military, attached to all 12 Panamanian ministries and five government-run institutions. US control, *Excelsior* added, extended to all of the country's cities and regions, and the Panamanian authorities 'frequently discuss their decisions' with their US 'liaisons' (whose names the paper gave). The Panamanian government denied the report.

Given the inequality of the relationship, in the economic as well as the military field, such discussions must inevitably involve a degree of pressure on the US side, even if only implicit. The Endara government asked for up to $2 billion in US aid to repair the damage to the economy and give it a 'kick-start'. Bush initially offered half that, but in the end Congress only approved $420 million.

In the meantime, Washington imposed its own demands on its new ally. Eagleburger explained, 'we look forward to co-operating very closely with the government of Panama in the important field of narcotics control. This will be a critical factor in our relations...' As early as 12 January the two governments signed a general anti-narcotics agreement, but subsequent negotiations on more detailed arrangements ran into Panamanian sensitivities about issues of sovereignty. Among other things, Washington wanted US coastguard boats to patrol Panamanian territorial waters, boarding and even sinking suspect vessels as required. The Endara government refused to accept this, especially when it was told it would have to pay compensation for any vessel the US unjustifiably sank.

This, and the even more sensitive issue of banking secrecy laws, became the major sticking points. Washington stressed that it would only deliver the aid package if the Bush administration could certify before Congress (as it is required to do annually) that Panama was 'co-operating' in the war on drugs.

The growth of the offshore finance industry in Panama depended to a large extent on the existence of banking secrecy — the ban on giving information to third parties regarding the relationship between bank and client. Even President Endara recognised that 'The success in the past 15 years of the International Banking Centre was due to drug money,' though this was flatly denied by Banking Association president Edgardo Lasso, who said the problem had been exaggerated.

US officials were not convinced that the Panamanian leadership had the will to modify the bank secrecy rules, especially given their own personal links with the banking world. Endara himself was a director of the *Banco Interoceánico*, allegedly a 'laundering bank', as well as being the friend and lawyer of Carlos Eleta, arrested in Miami on charges of smuggling 600 kilos of cocaine; Attorney-General Rogelio Cruz served as a director of First Americas Bank of Panama, a bank allegedly owned by Gilberto Rodríguez Orejuela, head of Colombia's Cali cartel; Guillermo Ford held shares in the Dadeland Bank of Florida, allegedly used by the Medellín cartel; and even Ricardo Arias Calderón's brother had links to a money-laundering bank.

None of these men had been convicted of any criminal activity, but their links to dubious elements in the banking community suggested that they might be less than objective on the matter. In September 1990, Rodrigo Miranda, a former special prosecutor dismissed some months earlier, accused Endara and other officials of direct involvement in money laundering — charges which, at the time of writing, have yet to be substantiated. Whatever the truth of this, if the government could not retain bank secrecy then the future of offshore banking in Panama — one of its main economic hopes — looked extremely bleak.

In March, the Endara government expelled Cuban ambassador Lázaro Mora, supposedly because his government had refused to recognise the Endara administration. Critics alleged that Washington had taken the decision as part of its campaign to isolate Fidel Castro, and pointed out that the move followed Vice-President Ford's trip to Washington the previous week to urge that the US speed up the flow of aid money. The expulsion raised serious doubts about Panama's relations with the Non-Aligned Movement, whose support had been important in the battle for revision of the canal treaty in the 1970s.

For many of Endara's opponents, Washington's 'hidden agenda' was to change the terms of that treaty revision and ensure a continued US presence after the year 2000. The truth seems to be a little more complex. Larry Birns of the Council on Hemispheric Affairs in Washington, an outspoken opponent of the invasion, said:

> 'I don't believe [it] was a ruse to prolong the US military presence. I believe the terms of the treaty will be fulfilled — although given Panama's economic situation they will negotiate a lease of some of their bases.'

Off the record, this is precisely what US officials say. Publicly it remains too sensitive an issue to be tackled directly. The official Panamanian line is that 'no new agreement will be negotiated to allow US troops to stay in Panama after the year 2000.' But many things can happen in the next ten years, and the crucial question for the US is whether or not it can ensure the continuance in power of compliant governments in Panama. In this respect, little has changed since 1903.

Public Force

In the aftermath of the invasion a large body of pro-government opinion, led by President Endara himself, immediately expressed a desire to follow the example of neighbouring Costa Rica and abolish the military altogether. Supporters of this view argued that Panama did not need an army to defend its territory, since it was bordered in the north by Costa Rica itself and in the south by the impassable Darién jungle. The 'third frontier' — the Panama Canal — was protected they said, by the provisions of the 1977 treaties: in other, words, any threat to it would immediately result in a US military response. With no armed forces, there would be no repetition of the coups which had marred Panamanian political life for the past half century.

Dr Juan Materno Vásquez, a lawyer and former justice and interior minister who helped negotiate the 1977 treaties, roundly rejected this argument. According to Dr Vásquez:

'If the amended constitution says there will be no army in Panama, you are then violating the canal treaty, because you are not assuming your part of the defence quota, which will be completely filled by the other partner... This is how we are going to see the military bases sneak in, because the US Army is then going to say that it requires installations to assume the unilateral defence of the canal ... because Panama does not have an army to do so.'

Nonetheless, the argument prevailed, supported by most ordinary Panamanians who had had enough of a corrupt and brutal military. The newspaper *La Prensa* argued for a total demilitarisation, including the eventual removal of all US forces. On 12 February 1990 the new government formally abolished the FDP. In its place came the new Public Force (FP), comprising the National Police, the Air Service and the Maritime Service. A constitutional amendment enshrined the demilitarisation principle: for the second time in its short history the Republic of Panama had abolished its army.

In 1904 the US had forced Panama to disband its fledgling armed forces and sign the Taft Agreement which formalised the position. In 1990 the US government, particularly the Pentagon, had reservations about the move. A small, highly-trained, professional army with a specialist canal defence role would have been more to its liking. Instead, it found itself training former FDP personnel to be policemen.

The dismantling of the FDP in a few short hours on 20 December 1989 left Panama with neither a police force nor an army. After looters had carried away virtually everything not nailed down (and quite a lot that was), the US forces began, rather belatedly, to fill the vacuum. Reluctantly, the government agreed to recruit former FDP members. It found the response overwhelming, and soon had a force of around 13,000, much bigger than at first intended. Ricardo Arias had originally stated that the new force would have only 4,000 members.

In response to widespread criticism that they were merely re-creating the FDP 'in different uniforms', the authorities protested that they had little choice. As Roberto Azbat, an aide to Ricardo Arias, put it, 'We did not want to see them become guerrillas. We wanted them to know that there is a place for them.' Equally important, he added, recruiting entirely from scratch would have meant accepting a US occupation for at least five years.

The US military assumed the guiding role, in this as in other areas of policy. Colonel Roberto Armijo assumed charge of the new FP. He was the only remaining member of Noriega's general staff and a man perceived by the Pentagon to be free from corruption. This illusion lasted less than a fortnight before the press discovered Armijo's million-dollar bank account, and he was unceremoniously removed from his post and placed under house arrest at Fort Clayton. He was replaced by his deputy, Lieutenant Colonel Eduardo Herrera, whom Noriega had fired as ambassador to Israel after he became involved in a US-sponsored plot. But the real man in charge was US army Colonel Al Cornell — formerly a military attaché in Panama, and more recently in Guatemala — now charged with the task of turning the FDP into the FP.

As the months went by, Panamanians grew increasingly worried by their new police force, staffed by the same, discredited people and trained by the US armed forces — the very body which had played the biggest part in creating the FDP. Many of the government's supporters, including leading members of the Civic Crusade, began to protest. 'They called the government,' said Alberto Conte, a Crusade leader, 'and said, "you guys have anyone who knows how to handle weapons?" "Sure, they're behind bars," was the answer. And now we have almost the same number of people, in fact the same people, as before. They are not creating anything, or filtering anything. They are reviving the old army.'

Even President Endara's spokesman, Louis Martinz, remarked that 'The same people who beat us are now supposed to protect us,' while Comptroller-General Rubén Carles, an ally of Vice-President Ford, said, 'Nowhere in the world has a corrupt military reformed itself. A corrupt army never changes.'

As a police force the FDP seemed virtually powerless to prevent a crime wave in Panama City. Murders, robberies and assaults ran at double the normal rate, spreading fear among Panamanians and US residents alike. In one well-publicised incident, thieves shot dead the chief financial officer of the Canal Commission in his home.

The FP's reputation was further tarnished in a case involving the kidnap for ransom, and subsequent murder, of the three-year-old grandson of Colonel Marcos Justine, formerly Noriega's chief of staff. Justine had managed to withdraw $80 million in cash from the National Bank just before the invasion, and had left some of it at the home of his daughter Guadalupe before his detention by US troops. Armed robbers had already stolen $350,000, and the kidnappers were after the remainder. Special prosecutor Rodrigo Miranda, charged with gathering evidence on Noriega's crimes, obtained information which implicated several former Noriega allies in the kidnap and murder together with leading members of the FP. They included Colonel Leslie Loaiza, now head of the Judicial Police and formerly an inspector in the FDP's security branch. Miranda was subsequently accused of irresponsible behaviour by Ricardo Arias, and sacked by the attorney general.

Seven months after the invasion an opinion poll showed that 75 per cent of respondents opposed the way in which the Public Force operated, and demanded changes. President Endara responded by saying, 'We will take into account all polls, opinions and criticism ... We must, however, act according to what we think is best while listening to the people's voices and criticism.'

Endara did not have long to wait before the discontent reached senior government circles. Responding in August 1990 to publicly expressed complaints by Arias Calderón over his performance in running the economy, Guillermo Ford told journalists that 'one of the most serious problems our country faces is the lack of public security. Just as the government [interior] minister challenged me to present my economic plan, I challenge him this evening to join our efforts to attain, once and for all, the security we need ... How can we develop our country's economy when we have not achieved social stability? I issue a call to the members of the Public Force, who should behave like men, not like pansies [*maricas*].'

Whether in response to this outburst or not, on the following day Endara telephoned Herrera in Miami, where he was on a private visit, and asked for his resignation. Herrera commented that the manner of his dismissal was 'not the most intelligent or objective'. His job was offered successively to four civilians, each of whom turned it down for what Arias called 'understandable personal and professional reasons'. The post eventually went to Lieutenant Colonel Fernando Quezada, leader of the abortive March 1988 coup against Noriega. Wishing Quezada luck, Herrera warned that 'serious confrontations are ahead of us,' an apparent reference to street demonstrations against the government, but a remark which could equally well apply to the increasingly acrimonious tone of inter-ministerial disputes. In September Quezada also lost his job, after he wrote to a local paper accusing its proprietor of incest. The paper had previously alleged that Quezada took drugs, and that he had accepted $25,000 from Noriega in 1988. Having exhausted its ex-FDP candidates for the post the government was reduced to appointing a civilian, Ebrahim Asvat, to replace him.

A Grim Future

The Endara government inherited an economy in shambles. Two years of US economic sanctions had cut Panamanian GDP by a quarter; the international banking centre had lost two thirds of its deposits; about 40 per cent of the workforce lacked steady employment; and total debts (internal and external) amounted to over $5.3 billion, including almost $2.4 billion in debt arrears. The government estimated the economic damage resulting from the combination of sanctions and invasion at up to $10 billion, and immediately asked Washington for $1.5 — 2 billion in aid. After some thought, the Bush administration promised one billion, and then set about the task of gaining congressional approval.

Ultimately, Congress approved $420 million in aid, a combination of loans, grants, credits, investment guarantees and other forms of assistance. The process was lengthy and disbursement of the money was slow and irregular. So slow, in fact, that in March the portly President Endara staged a two-and-a-half week fast 'in solidarity with the people of Panama'; and although he insisted that his action was not aimed at pressurising Washington, his protestations were widely disbelieved.

Area of El Chorrillo bombed by US stealth aircraft, which Washington claimed hit only targets with 'pinpoint accuracy.'   (Bill Robinson/*The Observer*)

As noted above, Washington made some of the aid conditional on certain actions by the Panamanian authorities, particularly in the field of anti-narcotics legislation. Roughly half of the second tranche of aid, for example, depended on the signature by Panama of a Mutual Legal Assistance Treaty, which would commit the country's authorities to supply documentary and other evidence required in narcotics cases, according to definitions of crime determined by the US.

The draft treaty was widely criticised in Panama as posing a threat to the country's status as a premier 'offshore' centre for paper companies, banks and insurers. According to the president of the lawyers' association, José Alvarez, it 'could destroy the Panamanian fiscal paradise', which had attracted 200,000 companies and 110 international banks.

The Banking Association agreed, in May, to report all deposits and withdrawals of more than $10,000, as done in the US. The uncertainty over what else it might have to accept contributed to the extremely slow recovery of international deposits.

Some suspected that the delay in releasing several million dollars' worth of canal tolls, held by the US under the terms of the economic sanctions imposed by President Reagan, also conveyed the message that 'business as usual' depended on an end to banking secrecy.

Neither cocaine trafficking nor money laundering showed much sign of having been affected by the invasion and the removal of Noriega — despite the fact that this was one of the major pretexts for military action. If anything, the rate of illegal drug shipments increased, according to local people. The State Department admitted that the lack of trained personnel and adequate planning meant that little had been achieved, even though there had been 'some progress' in terms of Panamanian government co-operation. The Colón Free Zone still laundered the proceeds of trafficking.

According to Rodrigo Arosemena, head of Panamanian customs, 'The size of the problem is really frightening. I don't think we, the US military or the DEA [US Drug Enforcement Administration] had any idea how much drug traffic was going through here.' This remark cast an interesting light on the much vaunted 'co-operation' which the Noriega regime had provided in the narcotics field up to 1987.

Former President of Panama (and World Bank official) Nicolás Ardito Barletta estimated that it would take the economy 15 years to recover to the level of 1988, and that the first task would be to generate 20,000 jobs in the next three or four years. But these jobs would have to come from private sector initiatives, since the government made it clear that the state sector would be drastically reduced. The government had no plans for major public works projects which could provide jobs and badly needed improvements in infrastructure.

After three months the Federation of Public Employees (FENASEP) complained of 8,000 redundancies; while despite budget cuts (blamed by the opposition on IMF pressure), the fiscal deficit was projected at $800 million, the highest in a decade. Guillermo Ford promised that the government would 'ensure the [job] stability of public employees, but in exchange for this we will demand greater efficiency and productivity.'

Already destined for privatisation were the national flag carrier Air Panama, cement, sugar and banana companies, and even autonomous institutions like IPHE, an organisation devoted to the rehabilitation of the disabled. However, the commitment to a '100 per cent private enterprise' economy within a year (to quote Vice-President Ford) was quietly shelved, with plans to privatise the electricity and telecommunications industries and the national savings bank dropped in June in favour of 'modernisation' plans.

At a workers' congress at the end of June, Mariano Mena, secretary of the Isthmian Workers' Central (CIT), said the government's privatisation schemes would give the private sector 'the key role in the government economy, and therefore the ability to manipulate the economic policy of the country.' This, he said, would 'leave the worker unprotected', and if these plans were not reversed 'the workers will take to the streets.' Plans to modify labour legislation, to make it more 'flexible', in line with the demands of the Chamber of Commerce also angered the trade unions.

The workers were not the only ones critical of the government's plans. In July the president-elect of the industrialists' union, SIP, wrote an open letter to President Endara in which he described the economic strategy as 'contradictory, confused and inconclusive.' Juan Ramón Feliú identified the major problem as the continued reliance on an outdated, services-led economic model. The government's proposals for privatisation, deregulation and export growth would do nothing, he said, to resolve the serious unemployment problem.

The dispute once more brought to the surface the historical problem of Panama, a country ruled by traders and middlemen with little interest in production.

Guillermo Ford pointed to predictions that the economy would grow by between six and seven per cent in 1990, but he omitted to acknowledge that much of this was attributable to the reconstruction required after the invasion, to companies re-stocking after the looting and to the one-off effect of the lifting of US sanctions. Steady, sustainable growth was something else, especially as foreign investors took their cue from the slow response by official donors and the unevenness of the return to political stability.

The agro-export industry benefited from the recovery of the sugar quota, although the international price of sugar promptly fell sharply. Bananas, which in the 1980s accounted for about $70 million annually in export earnings, had in any case been relatively unaffected by sanctions. There was little sign that the government intended to do anything serious about domestic agriculture, long a neglected area of the economy and one which could potentially provide not only jobs but an improvement in the trade balance.

On the debt front, Panama could eventually qualify for a debt relief scheme under the terms of the Brady Plan, named after US Treasury Secretary Nicholas Brady. But Washington made it clear that there would be no hope of this until the country cleared its $536 million in arrears to the multilateral lenders (the World Bank, IMF and Inter-American Development Bank). The government asked for assistance from the European Community and Japan, as well as setting aside money from US aid and its own unblocked funds, but by late August it still had not reached its target of $260 million from Japan and Europe.

Noriega in the Dock

One of the primary objectives of the invasion, according to the US government, was to apprehend General Noriega and take him to the US for trial on drug charges. US forces failed to capture Noriega, however, and on Christmas Eve he took asylum in the Papal Nunciature, the Vatican's embassy in Panama City. After protracted negotiations, he eventually surrendered to General Mark Cisneros of Southcom on the evening of 3 January. The prisoner was flown by helicopter to Howard Air Force Base, where he was put on board a C-130 transport plane and flown to Miami. On the plane he was formally arrested and his US legal rights were read to him in Spanish.

Noriega's arrest and removal to the US violated Article 24 of the Panamanian constitution, which forbids the extradition of Panamanian citizens. Although Washington has advanced legal arguments to suggest that certain treaties signed by Panama — notably the Single Convention on Narcotic Drugs (1961) — legitimise extradition in such cases, no extradition procedure was followed.

TV pictures of a manacled Noriega in the aircraft, and later of his official 'mugshot', complete with prison number, had a profound effect on many Latin Americans. As the Colombian magazine *Semana* put it, 'for many, that transfer went far beyond the limits of personal humiliation into the humiliation of a country, or even a continent'. In legal terms the action was unique. According to one specialist in international law, Professor Harold Berman of Emory University, the most recent equivalent was 'about 2,000 years ago. It was like the Romans leading back defeated leaders and taking them to the circus to be displayed'.

The Endara government, which began by declaring that it would not allow the violation of the constitution, ended by washing its hands of the affair on the grounds that its judicial and penal systems were in such disarray that they could not deal with the case. The Vatican too had initially suggested that no precedent existed for handing over an asylum-seeker to an occupying power, but eventually the nuncio, Monsignor Sebastian Laboa, collaborated in the plan to persuade Noriega to hand himself over. The general later claimed that he had done so only after the Panamanian government had threatened to remove the nunciature's diplomatic immunity, leaving him in danger of being lynched by angry opponents.

The manner of his arrest and the circumstances surrounding it became the subject of legal manoeuvres by Noriega's team of US lawyers. They argued successfully that the general was a prisoner of war, and as such entitled to wear his uniform and to enjoy certain other privileges. They failed, however, to have the case transferred to a neutral country under the terms of the Geneva Convention.

At a series of court hearings in Miami, where Noriega was formally charged on the basis of the 1988 Miami indictments, the defence sought to have the case dismissed altogether on a number of grounds. These included the illegality of the invasion in international law; the sovereign immunity of a head of state; the intimidation used to secure Noriega's surrender; and the violation of the 1977 Carter-Torrijos treaties, which require Panamanians arrested by US forces to be handed over to Panamanian authorities for trial. None of these arguments was successful.

Noriega was charged on a dozen separate counts of racketeering and corruption (to which the charges included in the Tampa indictment could later be added, along with any others the prosecution cares to bring). The main points are these:

● that he accepted $4.6 million in bribes from the Medellín cartel for protecting cocaine shipments to the US and money laundering in Panamanian banks;
● that he allowed Colombian drug traffickers to use Panama as a refuge and centre of operations during the 1984 crackdown on their activities by the government of their own country;
● that he travelled to Cuba in 1984 to seek the assistance of Fidel Castro in restoring relations with the cartel after he had ordered a raid on a large cocaine laboratory belonging to them (a point on which evidence may be presented by the Cubans themselves, who have promised to provide information for the trial);
● that he facilitated the shipment of chemicals needed for the production of cocaine.

The indictment names a total of 16 defendants, of whom six (including Noriega) are in custody. The cases could be heard separately if the court gives its permission, although the chances of this are not thought to be good. If found guilty on all the Miami counts, Noriega could face a sentence totalling 145 years imprisonment and a fine of almost $1.5 million.

The prosecution faces a number of problems in securing a conviction, however. Firstly, its case is largely, though not exclusively, based on the testimony of witnesses whose credentials the defence could place in doubt. Many of them are themselves convicted drug smugglers. Documentary evidence of Noriega's involvement in the trade has proved elusive: despite the huge pile of documents captured at the time of the invasion, the prosecution has 'found no smoking gun,' a US official in Panama said. 'Noriega was smart enough not to put anything on paper.' The only document so far thought to contain incriminating evidence is a letter to Noriega from convicted marijuana smuggler Stephen Kalish, in which he allegedly refers to tactics for dealing with Colombian cocaine traffickers.

The 50 kilos of 'cocaine' allegedly found in Noriega's home turned out to be as fictional as many of the other possessions given widespread publicity at the time — such as the 'fifty valuable oil paintings' which proved to be by virtually unknown artists. Analysis showed that the 'cocaine' was in fact the ingredients for making *tamales*, a national dish in Panama. Likewise, the precise ownership of assets, including property, boats and aircraft, attributed to Noriega, as well as the origin of the estimated $20 million in the 27 bank accounts initially frozen at the request of the Justice Department, has proved hard to determine.

The defence won one early round in the pre-trial battles when it forced the administration to unfreeze part of this money in order to allow Noriega to pay his legal bills, which could reach $5 million. The lawyers argue that much of the money so far traced (about $11 million) can be attributed to payments by the CIA and other US intelligence agencies, which they say totalled around $70 million. In support of this contention they have demanded that these agencies reveal how much they paid Noriega during the last 30 years.

Even if the prosecution can show that some of the money came from the drug trade, the defence may counter this with the argument that these activities were known to US officials and sanctioned as part of a broader policy. In this connection, Noriega's letters of praise from the DEA and others should prove useful. One reputation which may well suffer is that of the late William Casey, the CIA chief who had a fondness for off-the-record deals with dubious characters, and who could be accused of giving the green light for the general's involvement with the cartel.

This is not the only sensitive area in which the defence will have a right to seek documentary proof. According to the former prosecutor largely responsible for the Miami indictment, Dick Gregorie, they are entitled to ask for three main types of document: those which would tend to exonerate Noriega; those which would cast doubt on the credentials of a prosecution witness; and anything relevant to the specific charges. The trial judge must then determine whether the defence requests are reasonable: if the government then invokes national security in order to prevent disclosure in open court, this could lead to the dismissal of some or all of the charges.

This could cause serious problems for the prosecution. Many believe Noriega can embarrass George Bush — with whom his relationship dates back to at least 1976 — by revealing details of his possible involvement in the secret US war on Nicaragua in the mid 1980s. However, his lawyers will have to show that such information is relevant to the case before it can be used; moreover, since Bush emerged unscathed from the blood-letting within the US establishment over the Iran-contra scandal, it seems unlikely that the Noriega trial could damage his presidency.

Nonetheless, as a former CIA official put it, 'He can make us look terribly meddlesome. He can expose a lot of activities, people and places. At a minimum, it will be embarrassing and difficult. This sort of case is bad enough when there's nothing there. It's doubly bad if, as in this case, there is.'

As of the time of writing, the trial is set for 28 January 1991, although there is no certainty that preparations will be complete by then. When it does begin, it is likely to take five or six months and to cost the US taxpayer well in excess of $10 million. The greatest potential for political damage to George Bush arises not so much from courtroom revelations but from the possibility of an acquittal, something which can by no means be ruled out.

Conclusion
Made in the USA

As the first anniversary of the invasion approached, Panama had yet to emerge from the crisis created, in large measure, by the US confrontation with Noriega. Its economy was in poor shape and looked as if it needed at least a decade to recover. Its government was internally divided and rapidly losing public support, while the enormous influence still exerted over domestic policy by the US cast doubt on the international standing of the Endara regime. Common crime was at an all-time high, and the popularity of the police at least as low as under Noriega. The thousands of victims of the invasion had yet to be compensated or re-housed, and the precise death toll was still a matter of controversy. The persecution of the political opposition had been criticised by international human rights organisations, and street demonstrations were once more being met with birdshot.

None but a Noriega crony would have wished for a return to the years of military dictatorship, and few even troubled to mark the July anniversary of Torrijos' death. Washington and its long-serving 'asset' Noriega had combined to wreck Torrijos' dream of Panamanian national independence and prosperity.

The invasion's full implications go well beyond the immediate damage to the Panamanians' health, security and welfare, severe though this was. Hard to measure and more insidious is the effect of the poison injected into the body politic. The essence of a nation is not that it should fly its own flag or occupy a seat at the UN, but that it should create and reaffirm its own identity. Panama was a country carved out of the heart of Latin America to serve the objectives of a foreign power. The most important actor on the Panamanian stage was unquestionably Uncle Sam, and thus the swiftest route to political change has invariably passed through Washington.

The tradition persists, for whatever else it may be, the new government can claim no nationalist credentials. The platform on which the ADOC coalition fought the 1989 election gave it no mandate to take office on the coat-tails of a foreign military intervention, and indeed its leaders have often, though too late, sought to distance themselves from the invasion which put them in power. Foreign Minister Julio Linares told journalists in September 1990 that 'if we analyse [the situation] we must reach the conclusion that the US — of this I am sure — did not carry out its military action to liberate Panama but for reasons related to its own interests'.

The composition of the ADOC leadership — rich, white and linked to local and foreign finance capital — shows no break with a past in which the creation of a genuinely national economic and political programme has almost always been subordinated to the short-term interests of a clique of merchants, traders and financiers. The single, qualified exception to that historical pattern, the government of Omar Torrijos, has been repudiated by the new regime, which has sought to obliterate all trace of it.

The effect of all this on the self-image of Panamanians and the chances of creating a Panamanian identity can scarcely be overemphasised. Those who during the anti-Noriega demonstrations of 1987-89 pleaded with the US to intervene and rid them of the tyrant it had created bear a heavy responsibility. It is useless for them to attempt to shift the blame onto the Organization of American States for its failure to achieve a negotiated settlement: the fundamental failure was that of the Panamanian political leadership, which never showed itself able to find local solutions to local problems.

'"Help me, sir!" was the first cry of the "patriots" who had acclaimed the US army when it crushed Panama. The ruins of Panama City still smelled of corpses when the businessmen of the Civic Crusade began to dream of the "reconstruction business" they would create out of US aid', wrote Enrique Ortego of the CRIES think-tank in Nicaragua.

The net result is a crushing setback for those who would create a nation out of a geopolitical expression, a people with pride out of a piece of real estate. Torrijos' old friend, Chuchu Martínez, had often said that, 'this is a country of services, and a country of services unfortunately generates a servile mentality'. After the invasion he wanted to leave Panama: 'I feel old, for the first time in my life I feel depressed, humiliated, impotent, ashamed, my teeth are broken, I'm reduced to shit. I'm going to retire, I'm 60 years old and I've spent 30 fighting for my country'. In Martínez' view, Panama has regressed 50 years.

For Raúl Leis, Panamanian sociologist, 'we have seen a people who on being invaded take to the streets to loot instead of to resist; who then build barricades to defend private property and end up making friends with the invader and denouncing their neighbours'.

Leis hopes the world will learn the lesson, that the US will still flex its military muscle whenever it wishes, and that in a post-Cold War world, there is no-one to say otherwise. True, the communist bogeyman has proved a paper tiger, but drugs will do just as well as a pretext for intervention. The future prospects were summed up thus by Xabier Gorostiaga, a Panamanian academic and priest who has worked in Nicaragua since 1979: 'There is no end to the Cold War in Central America, no world-wide *détente* with the Soviet Union which reaches the "back yard". The Berlin Wall has fallen, but the US reinforces its wall of control and satellization in Central America.' Whatever form the next wave of resistance and struggle should take, it must surely involve the fight for sovereignty, national self-respect and freedom from Washington's dictates, for in the words of Simón Bolívar:

> 'Freedom is not, never has been and never will be a product "made in USA". For this reason we have never, nor will we ever, need to import it.'

Appendix I
US Violations of International Law

So comprehensive was Washington's disregard for the provisions of international law in its dealings with the Noriega regime that a separate book would be needed to do full justice to the subject. This brief summary, however, shows the range of violations and the threadbare nature of the Bush administration's post-invasion justifications.

The invasion

One of the fundamental corner-stones of international law is the doctrine of non-intervention in the internal affairs of sovereign states. This principle is enshrined in a large number of treaties signed by the US, including the United Nations Charter, the Charter of the Organization of American States, the Rio Treaty (Interamerican Treaty of Reciprocal Assistance) of 1947, the Declaration of Montevideo (1933) and even the 1977-78 Panama Canal Treaties.

The US invasion of Panama violated Articles 2(3) and 2(4) of the UN Charter, which prohibit the 'threat or use of force' and require disputes to be settled by 'peaceful means', as well as a dozen articles of the OAS Charter, most importantly Articles 18, 19, 20 and 21. Article 18 forbids intervention by any 'State or group of States..for any reason whatever, in the internal or external affairs of any other State', while Article 21 binds American states not to use force 'except in the case of self defense in accordance with existing treaties or in fulfilment thereof.'

Similar provisions are contained in Articles I and II of the Rio Treaty and Articles 5 and 14 of the Panama Canal Treaty, as well as in the Statement of Understanding appended to the latter. They are also embodied in a number of resolutions by the UN General Assembly, although the US claims these are non-binding. Mechanisms for the peaceful resolution of disputes exist within both the inter-American and United Nations systems.

If, after its brief and half-hearted attempt to resolve the dispute through the OAS, Washington considered this avenue to be closed, it was bound by the terms of the UN Charter to submit its grievances to the UN Security Council in order that a collective response could be organised. This it never did.

The US argument is that it was entitled to take action in self-defence under Article 51 of the UN Charter. It has used this justification for previous military actions, including the 1986 bombing of Libya in response to the death of a US serviceman in a supposedly Libyan-inspired terrorist incident in West Germany. But this argument requires an extremely broad interpretation of Article 51, the relevant part of which reads:

> 'Nothing in the present Charter shall impair the inherent right of individual or collective self-defense if an armed attack occurs against a Member of the United Nations, until the Security Council has taken measures necessary to maintain international peace and security. Measures taken by Members in the exercise of this right of self-defense shall be immediately reported to the Security Council . . .'

Most international lawyers take 'armed attack' to mean an attack on the territory of the state invoking the right of self-defence, and one which leaves no time to seek a peaceful resolution or collective action. It is clear from the language of the Charter that 'self-defence' is an interim solution to an emergency situation and that the threat must be genuine and the response proportionate. To suggest that the harassment, even the killing, of US citizens by Panamanian troops constitutes an armed attack requiring immediate, unilateral self-defence in the form of a 24,000 strong invasion force surpasses not only the terms of international law, but the bounds of common sense.

In a January 1990 letter to the *New York Times*, Alfred Rubin, of the Fletcher School of Law, stated that the fatal shooting of Lieutenant Paz on 16 December 1989 could in no sense be considered an 'armed attack' within the meaning of Article 51:

> '. . . just as the "rights" of foreigners to walk the streets of New York City do not justify foreign governments sending their own soldiers to keep order against American muggers or over-zealous American police.'

Another reason given by President Bush was that US troops had gone in to 'defend democracy', a somewhat absurd proposition, given the history of US relations with Panama, and one which is even less defensible in international law. It is, in fact, quite illegal for one country to intervene to change the government of another, regardless of how that government came to power. According to international law specialist Charles Maechling Jr, a former State Department official:

'This justification violates a basic tenet of the sovereign equality of states and arrogates to the user a right of political dictation hitherto claimed only by theocratic despots like King Philip II of Spain and communist rulers like Leonid Brezhnev.'
(*Foreign Policy*, Summer 1990)

Nor will it do to say that Panama had previously declared war on the US, since the statement by Noriega's rubber-stamp legislature that a 'state of war' existed did not constitute such a declaration. Indeed, the State Department did not use this argument, maintaining that the US troops had been invited in by the Endara government, despite denials by Endara himself and even though the invasion was under way before his inauguration took place.

US assertions that the invasion was justified in international law have no basis in fact. Rather, the attack was a unilateral action under the terms of the 1823 Monroe Doctrine, as elaborated on in 1904 by Theodore Roosevelt in what became known as the Roosevelt Corollary:

'Chronic wrongdoing, or an impotence which results in a general loosening of the ties of civilized society, may in America, as elsewhere, ultimately require intervention by some civilized nation.'

This doctrine, used to justify imposing US protectorates in Nicaragua, Haiti and the Dominican Republic earlier this century, is clearly unacceptable in the modern world, but it is the unspoken principle on which the US acted in December 1989. Roosevelt's words date from the time of the US creation of the state of Panama, suggesting that little but the language used has changed since then.

The pre-invasion period

US behaviour in the two-and-a-half years prior to the December 1989 invasion also frequently contravened international law. Its refusal to rule out military intervention constituted a 'threat of force', while the economic sanctions it imposed were forbidden, for example, by Article 19 of the OAS Charter, which states that:

> 'No State may use or encourage the use of coercive measures of an economic or political character in order to force the sovereign will of another State and obtain from it advantages of any kind.'

The Latin American nations were virtually unananimous in their view that US sanctions were indeed 'coercive' and should be lifted. They took this stance, for example, at the Latin American Economic System (SELA) meeting in March 1988.

The 1965 Declaration on Intervention and the 1970 Friendly Relations Declaration (both approved by the UN General Assembly) are among the international agreements which prohibit the use of economic, political or other forms of coercion to obtain from a state 'the subordination of the exercise of its sovereign rights'. The primary US objective at the time was the removal of Noriega as head of the FDP, and there can be no doubt that in international law the appointment or dismissal of a military commander is a sovereign right.

The decision by the US to withhold recognition of the Panamanian government following the removal of President Delvalle in February 1988 had no status in international law. Delvalle's 'government' (whose credentials were dubious to begin with) fulfilled neither of the standard criteria for international recognition: it did not control territory in Panama and was not in a position to fulfil the country's international obligations. For this reason, only El Salvador, whose government depended for its survival on US aid, followed the US line on Delvalle.

Curiously the State Department never claimed that the Solís Palma government (which succeeded Delvalle's) was itself illegal, only that it had taken office in violation of the Panamanian constitution. If applied impartially, this stance would require the US to withdraw its recognition from many governments around the world.

The post-invasion period

Even though neither side ever officially declared war, having opted to invade Panama the US became involved in an international armed conflict, to which the Geneva Conventions of 1949 applied.

In its May 1990 report (*The Laws of War and the Conduct of the Panama Invasion*) the human rights organisation Americas Watch found that US forces committed numerous violations of the Geneva Conventions. These included:

- failure to minimise harm to the civilian population
- failure to take adequate measures to collect and account for casualties
- exceeding the bounds of permissible action on the part of an occupying force in regard to searches, seizures and arrests
- failure to keep public order in the immediate aftermath of the invasion
- failure to meet obligations to civilians rendered homeless.

Americas Watch expressed its 'dismay . . . that the US forces are not conducting any serious examination of the weaponry and tactics used during the invasion to see if they violated fundamental rules of international humanitarian law.'

The organisation stressed that these were not minor points:

'. . . the laws of war are to be taken seriously. They are a prodigious achievement of humanity over many centuries and they result from a collective experience that has exacted a tremendous cost in human suffering. They are by no means "aspirations" or rules of thumb to be disregarded in the actual heat of battle, but enforceable standards of human conduct whose violation should bring about penalty and redress.'

The occupying forces' attitude to international law is nowhere better illustrated than in their treatment of foreign diplomats and diplomatic buildings. During the occupation, the papal nunciature, along with the Cuban, Nicaraguan and Peruvian embassies were surrounded by US troops seeking to capture Panamanians who had taken refuge in the buildings. The nunciature, where Noriega himself took shelter, was subjected to threats of forcible entry and to loud music from powerful speakers outside its walls.

A US tank pointed its gun at the residence of the Cuban ambassador, who was himself detained for an hour an a half, while the US troops raided the Nicaraguan ambassador's residence. These aggressive acts against diplomatic personnel and buildings violated the Vienna Convention, which covers the rights of envoys in foreign countries.

Finally there is the question of General Noriega's arrest, the primary objective of the whole invasion. Noriega left the nunciature and surrendered to US forces on 3 January, whereupon he should immediately have been granted the status of a prisoner of war. Instead, he was handcuffed and chained for a flight to Miami, where he was treated like a common criminal in clear violation of the Geneva Conventions. Only after the US court granted a defence motion invoking the Conventions were his rank and status respected.

The matter of whether Noriega can properly be tried in the US courts for crimes allegedly committed outside US territory is more complicated. The US Justice Department has stated categorically that the US has the right to apprehend criminals outside the national borders in cases in which the crimes affect US citizens or US national interests. But although there are some 'international' crimes, such as piracy or terrorism, which are recognised as being subject to 'international jurisdiction', it is by no means clear that the drug-trafficking offences with which Noriega was charged fall into this category.

Moreover, as head of state (until the invasion), Noriega should in theory benefit from the principle of sovereign immunity from prosecution. The US courts are unlikely to uphold this principle, even though immunity would automatically have applied if the crimes had been committed in the US by a Panamanian diplomat. One has only to reflect on Washington's likely reaction if any other nation sought to invoke a similar extra-territorial right to arrest US leaders to realise that, once again, the unspoken doctrine is 'might is right'.

Appendix 2
The Human Rights Records of the Noriega and Endara Governments

Noriega

Although the Noriega regime's human rights record has no bearing on the legality of the invasion, the US government has consistently argued that his violations of human rights made his removal from power not merely permissible but desirable. In August 1989, four months before the invasion, US ambassador Herbert Okun told the UN Security Council that:

'The Noriega regime's notoriety now rivals that of some of the worst dictatorships of this century, and justifiably so. This puppet regime has engaged in shameless acts of electoral fraud and manipulation to deprive the Panamanian people of the right to choose their own government. It is guilty of political murder and torture, drug smuggling, money laundering, gross violations of human rights, involvement in attempts to overthrow neighbouring democratic governments — the list is indeed appalling.'

For several years Washington singled out Panama for criticism over human rights, while systematically turning a blind eye to far worse violations in pro-US regimes elsewhere in Central America. To remark on this is not to downplay the importance of the violations committed in Panama, but to draw attention to Washington's double standards on human rights.

Panamanian governments have not traditionally resorted to political murder or 'disappearance' against their opponents. The State Department's own human rights report for 1989 (published after the invasion) notes that 'People in Panama seldom disappeared permanently under the Noriega regime'. The murder of Noriega opponent Hugo Spadafora in 1985 was a grisly exception, although there is also evidence linking Noriega to the murder in July 1971 of Father Héctor Gallegos, a radical priest. In 1988, according to the State Department, 'There was one known death as a result of political unrest' (a 26-year-old watchman who died of birdshot wounds thought to have been inflicted by 'pro-regime forces').

The situation deteriorated during 1989: at least three people died at the time of the May 1989 election, including Guillermo Ford's bodyguard, murdered by the Dignity Battalions, and an unknown number of FDP personnel were tortured and executed after the abortive coup on 3 October.

As the crisis worsened, from June 1987 onwards, human rights abuses proliferated. The government declared states of emergency, suspending constitutional rights to free expression, movement and assembly; it harassed or closed down the opposition media and prevented foreign newspapers from circulating. The regime even expelled some foreign journalists and prevented others from entering the country.

The General in his Labyrinth

It was Friday 13, the date which in Latin America concentrates all the evil omens. The full moon was just rising in the premature dusk of the tropics when the telephone rang in room 412 of the Marriott Hotel in Panama City. It was a functionary's dry voice speaking from the foyer, asking me to go with him to a meeting with Romero Villalobos, in the Ministry of Government and Justice.

Surprised, but still unafraid, I suggested that I would prefer to drive my own car to the meeting, at which point he told me that his orders were that I should go with him. I then asked him if he had a warrant for my arrest and told him that I did not have to obey him.

I phoned the Ministry of Government and Justice and managed to get hold of Mr Villalobos, who told me that I could either see it as an invitation or an order, but that I had to leave the hotel with the people who had come to find me.

I locked the door, put the security chain on and before I could think of what to do next the phone rang again.

— Antonio Caño?
— That's me
— Major López speaking
— Hello Major, how are you?
— Listen, you. You're a son of a bitch. What you've done to the *comandante*

has no excuse and you're going to pay for it. We have proof that you've sold yourself for 10,000 fucking dollars and you'll pay for it in jail. How could you do this to our *comandante* of freedom [*comandante de liberación*], with everything he's done, with what he's done for Spain!

— What are you talking about?

— Wasn't it you that wrote that article about the general in his labyrinth? [*El País*, 8 October]

— Yes, it was me

— And aren't you ashamed for having done this to a man who deserves better? You're going to pay for this. Are you still there?

— Yes, Yes, I'm here

— I'm going to play you our evidence that you sold yourself for 10,000 dollars. Just a moment. Hello?

— Yes, go on

— I'm a Panamanian citizen, with an identity card . . ., I am a witness to the way . . .'

I hung up, realising now that they wanted to do more than throw me out of the country. I phoned the Spanish ambassador, Tomás Lozano, who was in my room within 10 minutes. In those 10 long minutes, I had to calm the impatience of the soldiers in the foyer. I told them that Villalobos had said I had to leave the country and that I was packing.

Antonio Caño, *El País Internacional*, 23.10.89

Others were beaten up. According to the media monitoring organisation Article 19, under Law 11 of 1978 the Interior Ministry could:

'impose penalties without due process for distributing false information with intent to defame Panamanian authorities. Violations were punishable by fines, imprisonment, withdrawal of journalists' licenses and even the closure of print and broadcast media.'

Article 19, *Freedom of Information and Expression in Panama*, July 1990

Trade unionists were among those imprisoned for anti-government activities: in August 1980, 40 employees of the state power workers' union, including its general secretary, were briefly jailed for alleged offences against national security. They claimed their true offence was to have taken part in anti-government demonstrations. The government arrested more power workers the following month, but all were released by the end of the year.

The notorious 'Doberman' riot squads routinely broke up peaceful opposition demonstrations using tear-gas, birdshot and rubber truncheons. These tactics, not surprisingly, left hundreds of demonstrators injured. Those who came before the courts faced a system under FDP control. Judges were appointed, dismissed and transferred at the whim of the regime.

Concerned about the lack of due process and reports of torture (including beatings, electric shock and the use of knives and razor blades on prisoners' limbs), Amnesty International published a report in March 1988 entitled *Panama, Assault on Human Rights*. The organisation called for urgent government action to curb abuses, but received no answer.

The political campaign leading up to the election of 7 May 1989 was marred by harassment of opposition supporters and restrictions on opposition access to the media. On election day itself, vote counters were attacked and ballots stolen in an attempt to deny the opposition a victory which most observers put at around 3:1. The attempted fraud was more blatant and violent than in previous years, and it failed. The regime was eventually forced to annul the results and assume *de facto* power.

Nonetheless, fraud itself is nothing new in Panama. Washington willingly accepted Nicolás Ardito Barletta as winner of the fraudulent 1984 election, despite clear evidence at the time that the true victor was opposition leader Arnulfo Arias. According to John Dinges:

'The conclusion [of the internal US embassy study] was inescapable: Arnulfo Arias had been elected president by at least 4,000 votes, perhaps by more than 8,000. There had been ballot-stuffing, falsification of documents, systematic rigging of the vote count and a pattern of rulings by the electoral tribunal that ensured a Barletta victory.'
John Dinges, *Our Man in Panama*, 1990

In 1988 the US organisation Human Rights Watch published a report entitled *The Reagan Administration's Record on Human Rights*. In the section on Panama, the organisation condemned the superficiality of the administration's approach to the human rights issue, particularly over its insistence on supporting the fraudulently elected Delvalle after Noriega had removed him from the presidency:

'The Reagan Administration eschewed opportunities to take a stand for democracy in Panama at two earlier critical junctures: the 1984 electoral fraud that brought the Barletta-Delvalle team to office, and the 1985 removal of Barletta and promotion of

Delvalle to president . . . [and] when the Panamanian military committed its most heinous crime — the 1985 abduction, torture and decapitation of Noriega opponent Dr Hugo Spadafora - the Central Intelligence Agency chief in Costa Rica reportedly aided in the cover-up of the crime by providing a false witness (hired by the CIA) who appeared on Panamanian television blaming the crime on the Salvadoran guerrillas.'

Washington's sudden change of heart in 1987 was not so much due to the increasing brutality of the Noriega regime, as to the perception that Noriega had become a hindrance to US policy objectives. As long as he had been an 'asset' his crimes could be overlooked; now that he was a liability they would be subjected to closer scrutiny.

Washington has not only applied these double standards in Panama. Throughout the Reagan-Bush years the US has given an easy ride to regimes it sees as useful. The most outstanding example in Central America has been El Salvador, whose governments have been repeatedly certified by the White House as achieving improvements in human rights, despite the murder in the 1980s of over 75,000 non-combatants, most of them by the army, the security forces, or the so-called 'death squads' under their control.

State Department human rights reports strive heroically to avoid attributing blame for these deaths to the Salvadorean government, or even to the army and security forces, despite the overwhelming evidence collected by more objective human rights organisations. The Department's El Salvador report for 1988, however, conceded that the human rights office of the Catholic archbishopric of San Salvador attributed 89 killings between January and November that year to the security forces and 51 to 'death squads'. It also admitted that 'the officers of the armed and security forces are treated differently from other citizens before the law' and that 'No military officer has been convicted of human rights violations or any other crime in recent years.'

In November 1989, weeks before the US invaded Panama, the Salvadorean army murdered six Jesuit priests, their housekeeper and her daughter. Although nine soldiers, including a colonel, were subsequently arrested for the crime, the Church and other bodies have alleged that the officers who gave the original order have been protected. The US continues to provide around $1 million a day in aid to El Salvador.

Elsewhere in the region, pro-US governments in both Honduras and Costa Rica have been 'involved in attempts to overthrow neighbouring democratic governments'. Each of them played host for much of the

1980s to the US-backed contras who were seeking to overthrow the elected government of Nicaragua. If electoral fraud is the test, consider Mexico, whose ruling Institutional Revolutionary Party (PRI) has employed it for at least the last 30 years in order to retain its virtual monopoly on power. Washington rarely complains, content that the PRI provides 'stability' and prevents more left-wing parties coming to power by democratic means.

As Human Rights Watch noted in 1988:

> 'Because of its narrow focus, the Reagan Administration's campaign to pull the rug from under the feet of a long-standing dictatorial ally . . . appeared unlikely to transform a short-term change of power into a long-term commitment to human rights and democracy.'

Endara

From the moment it took power, the Endara government's attitude towards human rights came under scrutiny by local, regional and international bodies. Many of them expressed concern that, in some respects at least, there was a danger of replacing one wrongdoer with another.

Americas Watch, whose report was published in May 1990, spoke of the 'failure of the Endara government to follow the rule of law in the weeks immediately following the invasion.' It referred specifically to arrests and detentions of civilians on vague charges which often seemed part of a 'political purge' rather than due process.

In particular, it singled out Attorney-General Rogelio Cruz' decision to prosecute all the members of Noriega's Council of State, the short-lived body set up after the 1989 election. The charges were, according to Americas Watch, an 'impermissible extension by analogy of a criminal provision' (against using force of arms to prevent the exercise of its functions by a legally constituted authority).

The organisation added that 'these prosecutions are a powerful tool to prevent development of any significant opposition, at least from quarters sympathetic to the old regime.' It also criticised the prosecutions of former Dignity Battalion members merely on the grounds that they had belonged to the militia, which had been legal prior to the invasion.

Americas Watch attacked Endara's failure to purge the Public Force of human rights abusers, in particular the establishment of an intelligence and counter-intelligence office staffed by former members of Noriega's secret police. 'These agents,' said Americas Watch, '. . .

have already started arresting people without warrants or due process and bringing them in for secret interrogation.'

The media monitoring organisation Article 19 and the Inter-American Press Society (SIP) examined freedom of expression under the new regime finding that, in the words of SIP, 'the conditions have very much improved.' They too, however, found cause for concern in certain areas.

One involved the dismissal of 319 employees, including 79 journalists, by the *Panamá América* publishing house after it was returned to its previous owners, the Arias family. The military regime had taken over *Panamá América* and renamed it ERSA. After the invasion it was re-occupied, although the Ministry of Labour agreed to sequester its assets when the sacked employees filed a complaint. Several other media outlets were sequestered, pending decisions on their legal ownership.

The Journalists' Union of Panama (SPP), the only journalists' union recognised under the Noriega regime, has protested that its members have been subjected to political persecution since the invasion. The case of Escolástico Calvo, a journalist who managed the ERSA group until 20 December 1989, has been taken up by the SPP and human rights bodies. US troops arrested Calvo on 3 January and held him for 10 days at a US military detention centre before transferring him to the *Cárcel Modelo* prison. In July, Article 19 called on the authorities to release him or make known the charges against him.

Olga Mejía, president of the National Commission for Human Rights in Panama (CONADEHUPA), has alleged that she has been harassed by the US and Panamanian security forces and has received death threats.

According to CONADEHUPA, in June 1990 there were still more than 100 political prisoners who had been detained after the invasion. The pro-government human rights commission, CPDH, put the number at only one — a former member of Parliament, Rigoberto Paredes.

The Inter-American Human Rights Commission (CIDH) called in July for 'urgent and effective measures to resolve problems of human rights violations.' CIDH expressed particular concern over 'the situation of the prison population' and the 'lack of legal assistance'. Many of the prisoners, it said, were serving long sentences without being brought to trial and 'in many cases without the judicial process having begun.'

A member of the CIDH delegation added that there was 'a worrying situation as regards the condition of the refugees and the need to investigate disappearances, deaths and destruction.'

The Reconciliation Commission, set up by President Endara and headed by Archbishop Marcos McGrath, recommended in August that the 'US occupation should cease', that a full inquiry be conducted into the 20 December invasion, and that there be an amnesty for political crimes. The government, the Commission concluded, should avoid 'favouritism, privileges, nepotism and influence-peddling', and should ensure that justice was done.

Students and university authorities have also complained of harassment and violations of university autonomy. On 12 February, according to the University of Panama's rector, US troops entered the campus and broke into offices belonging to the associations of students and academics. The *Instituto Nacional* high school, which was closed down under the previous regime, was closed again in August after demonstrations against the expulsion of five students. In an ominous return to pre-invasion days, troops once again used birdshot against student demonstrators.

Further Reading

Tom Barry, *Panama: A Country Guide*, The Inter-Hemispheric Education Resource Center, Albuquerque, 1990

John Dinges, *Our Man in Panama*, Random House, New York, 1990

Frederick Kempe, *Divorcing the Dictator: America's Bungled Affair with Noriega*, G.P. Puttnam's Sons, New York, 1990

David McCullough, *The Path Between the Seas*, Simon and Schuster, New York, 1977

Graham Greene, *Getting to Know the General*, Bodley Head, London, 1984

Forthcoming: John Weeks and Andrew Zimbalist, *Panama at the Crossroads*, University of California Press, 1991

Periodicals:

North American Congress on Latin America (NACLA), *Report on the Americas, Panama: Reagan's Last Stand*, Vol XXII No 4, July/August 1988

John Weeks, 'Panama: the roots of current political instability', *Third World Quarterly*, Vol 9 No 3, July 1987

Andrew Zimbalist, 'The failure of intervention in Panama: humiliation in the back yard', *Third World Quarterly*, Vol 11 No 1, Jan 1989

Ricardo Arias Calderón, 'Panama: Disaster or Democracy', *Foreign Affairs*, Winter 1987/88

Charles Maechling, Jnr, 'Washington's Illegal Invasion', *Foreign Policy*, Summer 1990

Seymour Hersh, 'The Creation of a Thug: Our Man in Panama', *Life*, January 1990

Human Rights reports:

Americas Watch:
Human Rights in Panama, New York, April 1988
The Laws of War and the Conduct of the Panama Invasion, New York, May 1990

Amnesty International: *Panama: Human Rights Abuses in Connection with 7 May Elections*, London, June 1989

Article 19, *Freedom of Information and Expression in Panama*, London, July 1990

Latin American Human Rights Association (ALDHU)/Commission on United States-Latin American Relations, *Report of Joint Mission*, February 1990

Physicians for Human Rights, *Operation Just Cause: The Medical Cost of Military Action in Panama*, Somerville Massachussetts, March 1990

US State Department, *Country Reports on Human Rights Practices*, (Annual)

Index

Endara, Guillermo 13, 29, 74, 79, 89-91,
    93, 96, 99, 101, 102, 106, 110, 124-6
Esquipulas II 82
Europe 21, 28, 58, 63, 67, 105

FDP 3-10, 16, 17, 29, 39, 41-4, 55, 58,
    59, 63, 72, 76-9, 82, 84-9, 92, 95, 99,
    100, 116, 120, 121
FENASEP 104
flag riots 29, 35
FMLN 48
Ford, Guillermo 13, 29, 74, 79, 80, 89,
    90, 96, 98, 101, 104, 105, 120
Fort Amador 3, 8
Fort Clayton 13, 100
FP 63, 90, 99, 102, 124

G2 43, 47
García, Alan 91
García Márquez, Gabriel 31, 32
Gatún Lake 27, 68
Giroldi, Captain Moisés 86, 87
GN (National Guard) 30, 39, 40, 41,
    46, 47, 50, 52, 59
gold 19, 21, 34, 35
González, Felipe 85
Greene, Graham 30, 34
Grenada 10, 11, 48
Group of Eight 83, 92
Guatemala 13, 82, 84, 100

Haiti 20, 35, 115
Hay, John 23, 24
Herrera Hassan, Colonel Eduardo 77,
    78, 100, 102
Honduras 14, 49, 92, 123
Howard Air Force Base 3, 4, 65, 106
human rights 2, 13, 42, 57, 110, 119-26

independence 1, 14, 18, 20, 22, 23, 25,
    39, 110
IMF 104, 105
international law 113-8
Iran 76
Iran-contra 66, 109
Iraq 2, 76
Israel 41, 43, 48, 100

Japan 68, 105
Johnson administration 29, 36

Kennedy, President John 30, 34
Kissinger, Henry 37
Kuwait 2

Latin American Parliament 91
Linares, Julio 90, 91, 96, 111
looting 10, 89, 105

M-19 48
M-20 92-3
Machos de Monte 3, 87
Martínez, Major Boris 30-1, 46
McGrath, Archbishop Marcus 57-8,
    95, 126
Medellin cartel 52, 54, 98, 107
Mexico 40, 83, 92, 124
MOLIRENA 90
money laundering 52, 76, 98, 104, 107,
    119
Mutual Legal Assistance Treaty 103

National Assembly of Representatives
    15, 25, 30, 92
NATO 69
Nicaragua 36, 48, 54, 57, 64, 69, 83, 92,
    93, 109, 112, 115, 117, 124
Nixon administration 31, 51, 64
Noriega Morena, Manuel Antonio 2,
    4, 10, 12, 17, 18, 31, 66, 93
— army career 41, 44-50, 55, 116
— arrest/charges/trial 101, 106-9,
    118
— attempted destabilisation of 61-
    6, 69, 70-7, 81-8
— drug trafficking 12, 14, 51-5, 59,
    61, 63, 104
— elections 13, 14, 29, 55, 77-4
— head of state 15, 118
— human rights 59-60, 119-124
— intelligence activities 43, 44,
    47-50, 61, 78
— wealth 43, 47, 50, 55, 108
Noriega, Luis Carlos 45, 46
North, Colonel Oliver 49, 54

oil 32, 68, 69, 76
Operation Just Cause 11-17, 65, 71
Organization of American States 36,
    71, 80-86, 91, 11, 113

Panama -army 10, 23, 25, 40, 89, 99, 101
— economy 33, 58, 60, 72-7, 86, 89,

LAB BOOKS

Recent LAB titles, and those of related interest, include:

Grenada: Revolution in Reverse
James Ferguson

The first in-depth analysis of how the US has tried, and failed, to turn post-invasion Grenada into a showcase for free-market development. Contrasts the policies of the revolutionary period with the USAID-prescribed programme of privatisation and export-led growth.

'... offers a wealth of hard information and incisive observation... essential for understanding a new phase in US foreign policy and the current predicament of the region.'

150 pages £5.75/US$9.50 ISBN 0 906156 48 3 1990   Rickey Singh, *Caribbean Contact*

Honduras: State for Sale
Richard Lapper and James Painter

Traces the transformation of Honduras from banana enclave to the linchpin of US military strategy in the region. Analyses the elements which distinguish the republic from its neighbours and explores the reasons why endemic poverty has not yet generated violent social conflict.

'State for Sale provides a comprehensive introduction to Honduras and will prove a valuable reference as the conflicts in Central America evolve.'

132 pages £4.75/US$8.50 ISBN 0 906156 23 8 1985   *Amnesty!* magazine

Colombia: Inside the Labyrinth
Jenny Pearce

Although heralded as the region's longest lasting democracy, Colombia has also been the scene of extreme political and criminal violence which has given it the highest murder rate in the world.

Inside the Labyrinth explains the reality behind these contradictory images. It examines the historical basis of the country's two-party system and analyses the corruption and instability which have weakened the state. Exploring the economic and social forces which condemn a quarter of the population to absolute poverty, it examines the role of the political parties, trade unions, guerrillas and civic movements in Colombia today.

'Jenny Pearce has mustered a formidable amount of information... readers will be rewarded with illuminating accounts of The Violence and the rise of the cocaine barons.'

312 pages £10.00/US$19.50 ISBN 0 906156 44 0 1990   *The Independent*

Prices are for paperback editions and include post and packing.